Ghost St
of
British Columbia

For
Steven Christensen Shappka;
my newest inspiration.

Ghost Stories
of
British
Columbia

JO-ANNE
CHRISTENSEN

Hounslow Press
Toronto • Oxford

Ghost Stories of British Columbia

Hounslow Press
A member of the Dundurn Group

Publisher: Anthony Hawke
Editor: Nadine Stoikoff
Designer: Sebastian Vasile
Printer: Webcom

Canadian Cataloguing in Publication Data

Christensen, Jo-Anne
    Ghost stories of British Columbia

Includes bibliographical references.
ISBN 0-88882-191-3

1. Ghosts - British Columbia. I. Title.

BF1472.C3C56 1996   133.1' 09711   C96-930605-9

Publication was assisted by the **Canada Council**, the **Book Publishing Industry Development Program** of the **Department of Canadian Heritage**, and the **Ontario Arts Council**.

Care has been taken to trace the ownership of copyright material used in this book. The author and the publisher welcome any information enabling them to rectify any references or credit in subsequent editions.

Printed and bound in Canada

Hounslow Press	Hounslow Press	Hounslow Press
2181 Queen Street East	73 Lime Walk	250 Sonwil Drive
Suite 301	Headington, Oxford	Buffalo, NY
Toronto, Ontario, Canada	England	U.S.A. 14225
M4E 1E5	OX3 7AD	

CONTENTS

Acknowledgements

It is important to acknowledge that I did not write this book alone. I had help and support every step of the way, and I wish now to thank those who provided it.

Thank you Dennis, my husband, who is my partner in every way.

Thanks to my family and friends, who can always be counted on for their enthusiasm.

For all contributors who took the time to write down their personal experiences, then, at my request, often found *more* time to elaborate their accounts and search for accompanying photographs — and, for those guardians of our past; the many helpful folks employed at BC's museums, libraries, and archives — I am most grateful. You are the people who shaped this book.

My appreciation goes to Stoddart Publishing for permission to quote from one of their books in the story, "Grandmother's Visit." This tale is based upon a story originally written by Sheila Hervey.

And finally, many thanks to my publisher, Tony Hawke, who has been patient and encouraging, as always.

Introduction

I've always hated it when people ask me what I do for a living.

If you say you're a writer (and this may hold true for any slightly flaky non-nine-to-five occupation), people's eyes just sort of glaze over. Back in the days when I wrote advertising, I would add that fact so that the blank stare would at least be replaced with a look of thinly veiled contempt. ("Oh, so you *lie* for a living," one master of tact actually said. Ironically, he was in sales.)

But for the past few years, what I've been writing are these true ghost stories, so if anyone presses me to be more specific about what I do, this is what I must tell them. And if the eyes were glazed over to begin with, we're talking full-blown cataracts, in response to this.

I have to assume that most folks don't know how to comment on such a senseless choice of profession. As for those who *do* say something, they seem motivated by the subject matter, rather than the fact that I have written about it. Interestingly, the reactions vary wildly.

Religious conviction seems to influence the response — but I'm a little confused as to how. It leads some people to believe in the earthly presence of spirits, and others to adamantly reject such a possibility. Yet, both camps credit their faith as the source of their conviction.

A similar division can be found among those considering the possibility that their own departed loved ones may be lingering, in some form, among us. Some people are comforted and reassured by the notion; others are horrified by it, feeling that the person cannot be at rest if they remain earthbound in any way.

And then there are those who just find the concept of ghosts generally upsetting. If you are one of them — and I must confess, I find it strange that you're even reading this book, if you are — I encourage you to enjoy the stories simply as stories. After all, if there is a subject matter that falls into the "believe-it-or-not" category, this is it.

For the record, I do believe in ghosts. I have found it impossible to *disbelieve* the many credible, honest people who have shared their experiences with me. However — being a "collector" of tales, and not a paranormal researcher — I have no burning desire to convince the rest of the world. I just hope that even if you cannot believe in the phenomena, perhaps you can find value in the folklore.

But — love it or hate it, believe it or not — it would seem that, as a society, we can't get enough of these mysteries. The books we read and the television programs we tune to are so often of a supernatural theme, these days. The immense popularity of Stephen King, R.L. Stine, and shows ranging from "Are You Afraid of the Dark?" to "The X-Files" proves our fascination. (Incidentally, Gillian Anderson, who plays Agent Dana Scully in the Vancouver-produced "The X-Files" claims to have a bit of a true BC ghost story of her own. She and her husband moved into a house near a native burial ground, and immediately sensed that they were not the only occupants. "It was creepy," was her quote in the March 10, 1995 issue of *Entertainment Weekly*. "It felt like there was someone attached to me." A smudging ritual was performed, and Anderson now feels that whatever spirits were there have left.)

But while our curiosity regarding the paranormal seems to be on the rise, it's hardly a new interest. "The X-Files" is simply "The Twilight Zone" of this generation; Peter Straub, a current Edgar Allen Poe. Go back a little further, and you'll see that even Shakespeare knew the entertainment value of a good ghost.

While I scoured the province's old newspapers in search of ghost stories, I found local evidence of their enduring appeal.

Nearly forty years ago in Victoria, a writer for the *Daily Colonist* by the name of Bert Binny wrote a series of articles on local ghost-lore, containing one of the more interesting theories I've come across.

Binny was challenging the smugness of those who were inclined to deny the existence of ghosts, based on the fact that they had never personally seen one. "How do you know you don't see ghosts?" was the headline of Binny's response in the April 27, 1958, *Daily Colonist*.

> Quite frequently, people think they have seen ghosts which afterwards prove to be real honest-to-goodness human beings.
>
> But could not the reverse process also take place?
>
> Are ghosts always recognizable as such?
>
> Could not what looks like a real person actually be a ghost?
>
> Do you know by sight everyone who has died hereabouts during, for example, the past year? If one of their ghosts appeared on the bus, on Douglas Street or in Beacon Hill Park, would you know it for what it was or, being a practical soul, assume that it was real?

Food for thought — particularly since I am often asked if I've ever seen a ghost. Generally, I say no, but given this theory, who can tell?

After I tell people that I've never seen a spectre, I usually add that I would like to. But lately, I've been reconsidering.

Under controlled circumstances, it would be exciting. However, life is rarely a controlled circumstance, and being frightened or surprised in my own home is one experience I would prefer to live without. It's a fine idea by daylight, this wanting to witness an apparition, but past the so-called "witching hour," I begin to think otherwise.

This past January, I gave birth to a son and, as with most infants, for the first few weeks his preferred time to boogie was between 2:00 and 5:00 a.m. Being an early-to-bed type, it's a time of day I would never see under normal circumstances and, in those quiet, dark, lonely hours, my imagination kept me morbidly entertained.

I would wander through our rather old house doing the rock-and-bounce step familiar to parents worldwide, and every so often I would peek out the window of our front door to see how the neighbourhood was keeping. I always saw the same thing: parked cars, dark houses, closed curtains, no movement. It would have been slightly unnerving to see *anyone* on our residential street at those hours, but then I began to think, what if I were to glance out the window and lock eyes with someone coming up our front walk! That would be alarming, given the time. But what if I then noticed that this person, illuminated in the soft, slightly weird orange glow of the streetlights wasn't exactly walking, but *gliding*, and that there were no tracks in the snow because, well, his feet seemed to be a good three or four inches off the ground?

To quote a twelve-year-old movie, "who ya gonna call?"

The wildness of my imagination during these early morning hours convinced me that, despite my curiosity, I don't particularly long for eerie things to be happening in my own home. But that's exactly what most of the people who write to me have to deal with. Ghosts in their homes, spooky incidents in their places of employment, strange stuff occurring in the places where they are forced to be, every day. And, it is worth mentioning that many people have little or *no* desire for such adventure, controlled circumstances or not.

A woman named Sandy McCormick, who was unable to sit through the average horror movie, found herself living one when the cycle shop she ran in Courtenay turned out to be haunted. According to the Courtenay Comox Valley *Record*, Sandy's habit of working late and spending the night on a hide-a-bed in the back room ended soon after the slow, steady, disembodied footsteps began.

Many other people demonstrated their very real fear by moving to new premises — extreme measures, unless you truly believe the old place to be haunted. One family I interviewed for my first book, *Ghost Stories of Saskatchewan*, actually had a priest bless every room of their haunted house, then proceeded to bulldoze it and, for good measure, torch the debris. Want to know the scary part? It didn't rid them of the ghost.

This would be a good time to mention, however, that while seeing someone float through your living room or having your appliances act as though they have minds of their own can be obviously disconcerting, the majority of people I speak to are more awed than frightened by their experiences. For many, it becomes a rather special memory — something mystical; spiritual.

Some folks are accepting; some are not. Some are inspired; some, frightened. But the common denominator seems to be this: countless people in British Columbia have had experiences that they simply cannot explain. And while I conducted my research, I was struck by the absolute openness, sincerity, and generosity these people showed me. These were very personal experiences — in some cases, very few people were privy to the details, before now — and yet the stories were willingly shared and entrusted to me.

I was also impressed, once again, with the helpfulness of people in the province's libraries, museums, and newspapers. Not only did they provide valuable stories and story leads, but often went "above and beyond," as they say, in their efforts to assist me and enhance this book.

A. Burridge of the Salt Spring Island Public Library Association sent along this tidbit:

> If you are writing about ghosts, you may be
> interested to know that the unnecessary insertion
> of 'h' in ghost is due to William Caxton (1422-91)
> who thought the word ghost looked more correct
> than gost. Ghosh!

Zoe Stephenson, in reaction to my letter to the Greenwood Museum, was inspired to write this marvellous poem for the *Boundary Creek Times:*

Have you seen a ghost floating through your rooms?
A translucent, shimmering light?
Waltzing in step to a wistful old tune,
then vanishing out of your sight?
Or talk to a stranger on Copper Street
who smelled of dank, dead musty air.
A wispy mist creeping up from his feet
when you glanced back, he wasn't there.
Have you heard screams or bumps in the night?
The scraping of rusty old chains?
Strange eerie noises that numbed you with fright
but never could be explained?

When the *Lakes District News* printed my request for ghost stories, they admitted to their readers that they had one of their own! Mark Nielsen's column contained a strange tale of hollow footsteps, mysterious flooding, unexplainably strewn paperwork, and cold waves of air in the room that once served as a morgue, when the building was a local police detachment.

All these people were incredibly helpful. All the British Columbians who answered my request for stories were, as well. Together, they shaped this book into what it is — a combination of well-known folklore and intriguing personal accounts, which can now take their place as part of the province's social history.

That they are inextricably tied to our history is one of the great things about ghost stories. As Bert Binny so accurately acknowledged, back in 1958, "Our heritage would be lacking without them."

Here are the ghost stories that are part of British Columbia's heritage.

I hope they are to your liking.

CHAPTER ONE

The Mysterious Museums

If ghosts are a product of our history, one could assume that the province's museums are home to many a story-telling spectre.

Often, as with Craigdarroch Castle (see chapter 6), the museums themselves have dramatic pasts as private homes or public buildings of certain significance. In these cases, the events that have transpired on the premises may have left behind a psychic mark, and previous tenants may have stayed beyond their earthly lease.

In some cases, however, paranormal activity appears to come not from the building but from the artifacts housed within. This is not surprising. Some theorists believe that a beloved possession can quite effectively chain a spirit to this dimension.

Whatever the cause, the effects are fascinating. From five different British Columbia museums come stories that you won't likely hear on an average educational tour.

Mandy: Quesnel's Haunted Doll

On January 25, 1995, the *Quesnel Advocate* ran a small article featuring one of the artifacts at the local museum. Dry reading material? Hardly. In fact, it inspired nearly one hundred people in this small town to visit the museum and see the exhibit for themselves.

The attraction was Mandy — an antique doll with an unsavoury reputation. She came to the Quesnel and District Museum in 1991, via a donor who seemed anxious to be rid of her. Ruth Stubbs, the museum's curator, remembers the moment well.

"She practically plopped the doll down on my desk," she recalled, in the *Quesnel Advocate*. "The doll had belonged to her grandmother. She said that she didn't want her daughter to play with the doll because it was starting to disintegrate."

The woman's apparent revulsion was contagious — or perhaps Mandy was able to inspire such feelings — for as Ruth Stubbs accepted the 1920s-era toy, she felt distinctly uneasy.

Admittedly, the doll's appearance was somewhat grotesque. A severe crack in her head made one eye leer suggestively and quite independently of the other. The realistically painted features could, at a glance, give Mandy the appearance of a real, but terribly scarred, child. And it somehow added to the eeriness that the doll spent her first forty-eight hours at the museum shrouded in clear plastic, a measure taken to determine whether insects had infested her stuffed, cloth body.

[The total effect] "was creepy, to say the least," wrote Ruth, "but I thought it was a feeling that I just had."

Perhaps, but interestingly, many people had the same feelings when they looked at Mandy. While the doll still sat in the

When museum curator Ruth Stubbs first saw this antique doll, she had just seen the movie *Child's Play*. "The doll reminded me of Chucky," says Stubbs.

(Photograph courtesy of Quesnel and District Museum)

museum's workroom, covered in plastic, one of Quesnel's pioneers happened to see her. According to Ruth Stubbs, the woman stopped short, exclaiming, "Oh, that doll gives me the creeps!" As time went by, numerous people — including all of the museum staff — admitted to being distinctly uncomfortable around the mysterious antique. And the collective intuition became difficult to ignore when strange things started to happen around Mandy.

All artifacts that come to the Quesnel and District Museum are photographed, and Mandy was no exception. The museum's photographer and her boyfriend recorded the doll in a number of different positions. They both reported feeling uneasy, but the photo shoot was uneventful. The next day, however, they entered the photo lab and found it in extreme disarray. Small items had been tossed around the room; pens and pencils were scattered across the floor. It looked, according to Ruth Stubbs, as though "a small child had had a temper tantrum." Later, the photographer went into the darkroom to develop the pictures. Shortly thereafter, she emerged from the room, looking pale and shaken. Ruth explained in the *Quesnel Advocate* that the woman had been working when "she heard a deep sigh behind her, and something fell off the shelf."

Perhaps Mandy is camera-shy, for the museum photographer was not the only one to run into problems. Ruth Stubbs invited a man from the *Cariboo Observer* to take some pictures of the doll. Afterward, the fellow reported that his effort had been a waste, as the contact sheet was chewed up in the developer. He told Ruth it was a strange incident; something that had never happened before, and had not happened since.

Even reporter Seth Gotro, of the *Quesnel Advocate*, wrote of his unusual experience photographing Mandy:

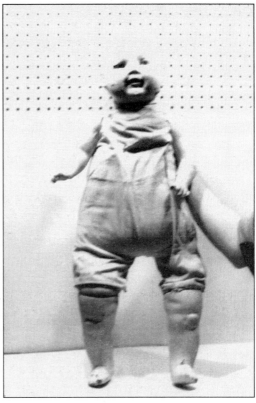

"When we started taking pictures of the doll with no clothes on, she began to look like a boy," Ruth Stubbs told the *Quesnel Advocate*. "It almost looked like a real baby."
(Photograph courtesy of Quesnel and District Museum)

When I photographed Mandy for this article, I almost swore she turned her head away from the lens so that I might not get her on film. When we took her out of the glass case and sat her on the bed, she seemed to be grinning at me as the flash hit her face.

Mandy inspired these strange feelings in nearly everyone who laid eyes on her. And the feelings, Ruth Stubbs believes, led naturally to the stories.

According to hearsay, the doll's glass eyes will follow a person around the room. Since her appearance, she has been blamed for a number of artifacts that have gone missing, then later turned up elsewhere. And then there's the most sensational story to have found its way to Stubbs; the one claiming that the doll was once dropped, and real blood came out of the cracks in her head.

While claiming not to believe the stories, Ruth Stubbs was admittedly curious. A retired curator from Surrey managed to fan that flame of curiosity when he visited the Quesnel and District Museum and held Mandy in his hands. The man was known for his ability to touch artifacts and pick up "vibes." What he felt from Mandy was that the doll had seen a great deal of abuse in its lifetime. Stubbs also added that when touching the doll, he got very cold chills running through him.

The retired curator's findings finally prompted Ruth Stubbs to return to the doll's donor for more information. She learned that the doll had been stored in the basement of the woman's home, and that some disturbing things had happened there.

"She told me that she kept hearing a baby cry in the basement," said Stubbs. "When she would go down, the window of that room was open, with the breeze blowing the curtains — but no baby. Now, this is what she *told* me," Stubbs qualified cautiously, adding, "True? Who knows."

Ruth Stubbs is always quite careful to point out that Mandy's unsavoury reputation is really the product of folklore —

and that there is no proof to support the theory that the doll is haunted. Still, as she explained to Seth Gotro of the *Advocate*, her own feelings are undeniable.

> Yes, I get a feeling from Mandy ... People will think I am crazy, but I think she is a lot happier now. That doll gave me the creeps when we first got her in. Maybe I'm just used to her now. I'm not saying the doll is haunted, but artifacts can tell a story by themselves.

Considering the strange, distasteful feelings she inspires, perhaps Mandy's story is one that's better left untold.

From Gold to Ghosts: The Black Nugget Museum

Kurt Guilbride is the private owner and operator of the Black Nugget Museum in the island community of Ladysmith.

Recently, a visitor informed Kurt that while she had been browsing through his vast collection of antiques, she had enjoyed a lively conversation with an elderly native woman. Not an unusual occurrence — unless you consider that the visitor claimed to be a spirit channeler, and said the woman whose

The Black Nugget Museum in Ladysmith houses an impressive collection of antiques and memorabilia — and perhaps a ghost or two from its own colourful past.

(Photograph courtesy of Kurt Guilbride, the Black Nugget Museum)

company she enjoyed was there because her remains, on display in a native coffin-box, are one of the museum's exhibits.

Now, that *is* unusual, and certainly interesting, but since buying this piece of history in 1972, Kurt has learned to take such things in stride. "This place is well over 100 years old," he explained on the telephone one day, "so several people have died here." He believes the Black Nugget's colourful history provides natural inspiration for such stories, and perhaps a favourable climate for an authentic ghost or two, as well. Kurt's own experiences have effectively convinced him not to dismiss anyone's strange tales regarding the Black Nugget.

The history behind all the stories and experiences began in 1881, when the Miners' Hotel was built in the town of Wellington. The proprietors were Sarah and Lodwick Jones — savvy, Welsh-born entrepreneurs who knew an opportunity when they saw one, and soon saw one in the booming coal town of Ladysmith. In 1900, they moved their hotel to Gatacre Street in Ladysmith and rechristened it as their namesake. The Jones Hotel welcomed new business in a new town, and went on to provide some flash and colour to the local history.

Sarah was a meticulous woman who kept the dining room and guest quarters in perfect, polished order but, in those wild mining days, the barroom — which was Lodwick's domain — commanded greater attention.

Lodwick Jones was an affable tavern host who kept a silver dollar in his pocket and routinely used it to flip the guests "double-or-nothing" for drinks. The atmosphere was pleasantly raucous, the drinks flowed freely, and so, too, did the money. Slot machines and card games dominated the room and the saloon became well-known as a gambling centre. In fact, it was during a poker game "gone wrong" that the Jones Hotel claimed its first violent death. A player who tried to better his odds by cheating was discovered; shot by his opponent, he died in a pool of blood on the barroom floor.

Did the unlucky fellow who lost the game in such an ultimate fashion make the hotel his eternal home? No one can say for sure — but perhaps the ghostly footsteps that are occasionally heard on the staircase belong to him: a tired card-player wanting to retire to his room and try his luck another night.

In the fall of 1908, the Jones Hotel again contributed a chapter to Ladysmith's history when Lodwick unknowingly precipitated what may have been the shortest gold rush in history. Two local men excitedly staked a claim on Gatacre Street after finding a small piece of gold in the sand. Hopeful prospectors poured into town, and the local newspaper published photographs of the crowds and headlines proclaiming that the streets were literally paved with gold. The excitement ended on a disappointing note when it was learned that the barroom mirrors at the Jones Hotel were being decoratively trimmed in 24-karat gold. A tiny piece of this trim, en route to the hotel, was accidentally dropped on Gatacre Street.

Have the spirits of some frustrated miners remained to drown their sorrows while staring into that gold-trimmed mirror? There's no doubt that they'd feel at home, leaning on the edge of the original bar, with its polished brass footrail.

Sarah and Lodwick continued to run their hotel until 1926 when they died — only a week apart from each other — in the bedroom they had shared for so many decades. Others continued to run the hotel successfully, until the late 1930s. By then, the Depression had taken its toll, Ladysmith's population had shrunk, and the hotel that had been so much a part of its adopted town closed. It passed through at least two owners, over the years, until Kurt Guilbride bought it in 1972, restoring it and opening it to the public as the Black Nugget Museum.

The rooms that Sarah and Lodwick Jones used as living quarters are among those that have been lovingly recreated by Kurt, and it is in one of these rooms that he feels their spirits may remain.

On the fireplace mantle in the drawing room is a parade of elephant figurines, various sizes, all facing east. Usually. But, every once in a while one of the figurines will turn 180 degrees and face west — without being touched. According to the February 21, 1995 edition of the *Ladysmith-Chemainus Chronicle*:

In what was once the Jones' own drawing room, one of the elephant figurines decorating the mantle will spin around — when the spirit moves it.
(Photograph courtesy of Kurt Guilbride, the Black Nugget Museum)

Guilbride first noticed the oddity when he returned after being away for several weeks. He turned the elephant back to the east and went upstairs to his living quarters. The next morning, it was turned back to the west again.

It happened fairly regularly after that.

It's a small thing, but perhaps enough to make one believe that Sarah and Lodwick are still keeping a ghostly finger in their business. Along with the phantom footsteps frequently heard on the stairs and the occasional visitor conversing with spirits, it seems certain that the Black Nugget Museum is housing more than just "physical" history.

A Greenwood Ghost Named "Charlie"

Greenwood, British Columbia, is officially on record as being the smallest city in Canada. This is based on an earthbound population of roughly one thousand people, but anyone who ever worked in the old museum knows that there are certain other-worldly types who also call Greenwood home.

For the past fourteen years, Greenwood Museum has enjoyed the privilege of its own facility — one that, to date, seems unoccupied by anything paranormal. Between 1967 and 1982, however, the museum was a tenant in Greenwood's old court-house and the supernatural situation was quite different.

The Greenwood Court-house was built in 1902, and cases were heard there for seventy-seven years afterward. But of all the dramas that played in that building, one is recalled above the rest.

It was July of 1915, and a man being held in a basement jail cell hanged himself. Perhaps the reason it seems so hard to forget this sad scenario is because many believe the doomed man's spirit never left.

According to former museum employee Zoe Stephenson, the ghost of the old court-house was known to all as "Charlie," and there are records of his antics disturbing several different people.

Although Charlie's presence was never particularly threatening toward his human companions, there was a museum manikin to which he took a particular dislike. On one occasion, a city clerk heard water running into a bathtub located in a back room of the museum. Upon investigation, he found the room deserted, the water still running, and the head of this manikin bobbing helplessly in the tub. The clerk rescued the head and it was reattached to its body, but Charlie was not about to give up.

On July 6, 1915, a man hanged himself in the basement jail of this building. To this day, many believe that "Charlie" remains there, in spirit.

(Photograph courtesy of Greenwood Museum Association)

Shortly after the aborted attempt to drown the model, Charlie succeeded in knocking her head clean off her shoulders. The curator arrived at work one morning to discover the ghost's handiwork; namely, the manikin's head smashed to pieces on the floor.

Although Charlie had also been accused of shattering an ashtray to frighten a woman who was working alone in the museum at night, he was generally a well-behaved spectre whose antics, while curious, were not menacing.

The ghost's footsteps were frequently heard wandering through the courtroom, long after closing. Perhaps he was re-living the trial he missed, or the one that went badly for him. In the museum, newspaper racks often clicked together, as if invisible hands were perusing the periodicals. It could be that Charlie was looking for the headlines that his suicide surely garnered.

Interestingly, one former curator of Greenwood Museum who dealt with Charlie by day had a ghost of his own to put up with at night. To make events even more confusing, the apparition in the curator's home bore a startling resemblance to his wife.

She was first seen by a friend of the family, who thought she was being rudely ignored by the lady of the house. The woman walked down the stairs, directly past the friend, and into the kitchen without so much as a "good morning." The insulted friend followed right behind, only to find the kitchen empty. Her bewilderment grew when she later found the curator's wife still sleeping in bed, having not been downstairs since the previous evening.

This mysterious double was also seen by the curator himself. On one occasion, he was quite shaken to see his "wife" rocking in a chair on the main floor, when he knew she was busy upstairs and, in fact, could hear her footsteps directly above him.

Could this have been the woman's double? ... known as a "doppelganger" in German stories, or a "fetch" in Irish lore? Such an apparition was frequently — but not always — interpreted as an omen of death. Thankfully, on these occasions, the double seemed to be on a harmless mission.

There were other forces in the curator's home that could not be seen. He would often lie in bed and feel the mattress depress as someone sat down on the opposite side. The man would turn, expecting to see his wife, and find himself alone in the room.

Happily, the invisible presence twice turned out to be a protective one. Cleaning up after a fire, the curator was carrying a mattress downstairs when he reached out to steady himself on the hand rail. He was surprised to feel a strong force pushing his hand away from the railing, and grateful when he later discovered the fire had left it loose and unsafe.

On another occasion, the curator's wife, responding to a strange feeling that she had, strongly warned against turning on a particular light switch. A subsequent investigation showed the wiring connected to that switch to be faulty.

It seems the ghosts associated with Greenwood Museum and its employees can be as helpful as they are fascinating.

The Chilliwack Legend

It would seem that suicidal prisoners are a busy lot in the afterlife. One of the most enduring bits of local folklore from Chilliwack begins, as the Greenwood Museum story does, with a jailed man taking his own life.

Chilliwack City Hall, shortly after its completion, circa 1912 — long before it became a museum and one of Chilliwack's favourite "haunts."

(Photograph courtesy of Chilliwack Museum and Historical Society)

It was about 1928, and the building which now houses the Chilliwack Museum was then City Hall. A man named Wilfred Garner had been picked up for drunkenness and thrown in a basement jail cell for the evening to "sleep it off."

Shortly after he passed out, the police brought Wilfred a room-mate; a Chinese fellow who was depressed enough about his situation to want a permanent solution. In an oral history recorded for the Chilliwack Museum and Historical Society Archives, Wilfred Garner's cousin, Samuel Roy Cromarty, relates his version of the story:

> They never bothered to take Wilfred's belt away from him, or anything, and during the night, that little Chinaman, I guess he decided that he didn't want to be taken up in front of the judge on account of an opium rap, so he hung himself with Wilfred's belt. Just how, it was hard to say. Well, he wouldn't hang himself, he just *strangled* himself.

Years later, Roy Cromarty was employed as a custodian in the very building where his cousin had once awakened to something worse than the hangover he was expecting. Roy told others that he had never worked in a building that made so much noise. There were creaks and groans and the loud complaints of expanding and contracting pipes. And there was something he couldn't quite explain — the sounds of other people, when Roy knew that he was very alone.

Footsteps would cross the floor upstairs, and a door would open and close. Sometimes the door would be heard first, and the footsteps would follow. Every time, Roy would rush upstairs to see who might be there and, every time, he was greeted with an empty building and a door that remained locked by a deadbolt from the inside. On other occasions, Roy would hear the sound of the back door opening and closing — but while the sound could be clearly heard, the door remained firmly shut.

At first Roy was reluctant to believe his eyes and ears, and he looked for logical explanations. He first thought the natural noises of the building might explain his experiences, but had to eventually admit that the footsteps were too regular and too many (up to twenty in a row) to be an illusion created by an ancient heating system and settling foundation. After another person witnessed the sound of the ghostly walking with him, Roy was more able to accept his own senses, and talk about the experience. He even had an explanation.

"I still think my little Chinaman is here, looking for a way out," Roy theorized, recalling the story of the disconsolate prisoner. "At least that's my opinion, and I'm gonna stay with it."

Although there is no evidence linking the two events, Roy Cromarty's explanation of the spectral footsteps has become a well-established and accepted story. The hapless Chinese prisoner who roams the Chilliwack Museum is now part of local folklore.

Rudolph Schultz: The Creston Crypt-Keeper

In terms of sheer entertainment value, the finest ghosts are made of people who were known for their eccentricities while alive. And in terms of eccentricity, one would be hard pressed to find a more interesting character than Rudolph Schultz, the Russian immigrant and master stonemason who spent his last years creating the unique building that is now home to The Creston Valley Museum.

Rudolph came to Canada in 1951 and, in 1952, purchased a piece of land overlooking the Creston Valley. The next fifteen years were devoted to the man's dream home. Rudolph Schultz's house was intended to be a showcase of his talents; a rambling structure of varied styles and designs, with walls more than eighteen inches thick, a working fountain, and several hewn-stone fireplaces. Everything was built from indigenous rock and locally scavenged items. The timely construction of the Kootenay Pass provided Rudolph with most of the stone. Windshields, salvaged from a variety of automobiles, made up the windows in the back rooms. And, never one to be wasteful or superstitious, Rudolph even employed the bases of crumbled tombstones in his design.

The stone house was in a constant state of construction; Rudolph meant it to demonstrate all his craftsmanship and skill. But anyone who ever came into contact with the somewhat reclusive Schultz remembered him as much for his idiosyncrasies as his talents.

According to Lois Price of the Creston and District Museum and Historical Society, everyone who knew Schultz had a story to tell about him. People recall him living on a diet of three staples: garlic sausage, fresh garlic, and wine. Rumour has it that Rudolph grew the garlic bulbs in his garden and brewed the

31

Rudolph Schultz spent his last fifteen years creating a masterpiece: the eclectic stone house where he hoped to spend eternity.
(Photograph by H.M. Buckna; courtesy of the Creston and District Museum and Historical Society)

wine in his bathtub. It was said that he never bathed, so the tub was always free for wine-making.

Considering Rudolph Schultz's personal habits, it was perhaps just as well that he didn't care for women. If they were dressed appropriately (to Rudolph, that meant a properly feminine dress or skirt), he would allow them in his house to view his different styles of stone work. However, he would never do business with a woman. Her husband had to be the one to make a decision and conduct the transaction. And once money changed hands, it stayed with Rudolph. He distrusted banks and carried a thick roll of cash wherever he went.

Rudolph's strange ways meant that he had no close friends, but he didn't seem to mind. His devotion was to his house. The man put his heart and soul into the great stone display — and apparently planned to do exactly the same with his physical remains.

The strange old craftsman built a crypt under the floor of one of the main rooms of the house, with plans to spend eternity there. Apparently, this was accepted in his native Russia and Germany, and it was a shock and a disappointment for Schultz to discover that it was not permitted in Canada. Reluctantly, he filled in the crypt. Rudolph Schultz, master stonemason, would have to be buried in a common cemetery like everyone else.

In June of 1967, after fifteen years of continuous construction, death forced Rudolph to abandon his beloved project. He was only sixty-five years old.

It is said that Schultz wanted the house to some day become a museum and, in 1982, The Creston and District Museum and Historical Society combined donations, private pledges, and a bank loan to purchase the unique property. Volunteers laboured to ready the building, stripping away the renovations of previous owners and restoring it to Rudolph Schultz's original vision. On September 12, 1982, The Creston Valley Museum opened to the public. Some said that Schultz should have been there to see it. Some others were beginning to suspect that he was.

Part of the restoration involved uncovering the original stone floors, which had been hidden since Rudolph's death by an inch of concrete and wall-to-wall carpeting. The workmen who chipped patiently away at that concrete were the first to feel that there was a supernatural presence keeping them company.

As they worked, both men swore they could hear a voice — Rudolph Schultz's voice — speaking in low tones behind them. When they would set down their tools and become quiet, in an effort to listen, Schultz was suddenly silent, too, making it impossible to catch his actual words.

The workmen also discovered that their ghostly companion left behind an odd physical mark. Each morning, there would be a mysterious white fuzz covering the area they had worked on the day before. It was never explained and, to this day, the white fuzz appears in the museum — but only over the floor crypt that Rudolph unhappily filled in so many decades ago.

Lois Price of the Museum and Historical Society explained that from these first "experiences" with Schultz, the legend of his haunting grew. To many, it was just a lively story, one that was fun to tell the tourists. Others, however, were affected more personally. In February of 1995, Lois wrote:

> Although we always laugh about Rudolph haunting our Museum, I have discovered since that there have been people who have quit guiding because of the haunted museum, others who will not be in the museum alone.

One woman who used to guide at The Creston Valley Museum quit after complaining that Schultz was following her around. She was quite sure it was him, as he had once been a patient at the hospital when she worked there. In that time, the woman came to know him by his peculiar scent — the famous, strong combination of garlic and wine.

The most frequent anomalies are small ones; lights that turn on by themselves, and doors that are found unlocked and ajar, after volunteers swear they've been secured for the night. The security alarm sounded late one night, due to an opened door which can only be unlatched from the inside of the building. These are relatively insignificant incidents, but together they have created a feeling of uneasiness so prevalent that a museum manikin had to be moved from its location by the door because jumpy staff members were repeatedly startled by it.

Lois Price acknowledges that almost any of Schultz's "ghostly activities" can be explained in logical terms, if one tries hard enough. Still, there are those who swear they have felt the eccentric stonemason's presence.

When a chill runs through The Creston Valley Museum late at night, and the air carries a pungent, unexplained odour of garlic and wine, it must be easier to believe what is nearly unbelievable. Rudolph Schultz's remains may lie in an ordinary cemetery, but his spirit has chosen to stay in the unconventional stone house that he designed to be his final resting place.

CHAPTER TWO

Three Stories from a "Sensitive"

Although it seems that nearly everyone encounters the supernatural at some point in life, certain people appear to be more sensitive than others. It follows that those individuals are either consciously aware of, or somehow attract, more than their share of first-hand paranormal experiences.

Shortly after I began corresponding with Moira Pitt, it became obvious that she was one of these specially gifted people. She had twice shared homes with former ghostly occupants — and had a history of receiving "messages" that went back as far as childhood.

"I just always knew things," Moira wrote to me. "I knew who I could trust and who not to."

Despite this helpful talent, Moira claims to have made the same mistakes as everyone else — perhaps because, in her conservative family, psychic powers were as vehemently denounced as they were plainly apparent.

Moira's religious paternal grandmother claimed to receive her messages "in prayer." Her mother had obvious abilities, but denied it. A great-aunt who embraced her gift and became a tea-leaf reader was considered too eccentric to bear and, so, was shunned by the family. Moira learned to keep her intuitions and messages to herself.

Still, whether she shared them or not, they kept coming. And whether she chose to acknowledge it or not, Moira was, by her own definition, a "sensitive." Her life was destined to be filled with unique experiences that some people will never understand.

The Walker

When Moira Pitt was a young girl, telling ghostly tales was a favourite way to pass the time.

"That was the only fun we had after dark," she wrote, adding that at that innocent time of life, she and her friends had yet to find "anything so exhilarating as our wicked ghost stories."

But no matter how great her interest in ghost *stories*, it would be thirty years before she met her first ghost — on a beautiful old dairy farm on Vancouver Island.

It was the mid-1970s, and Moira was a grown woman with five lively children of her own when it began. The Pitts had just purchased the dairy farm and found it perfectly suited to their needs. Moira noted that with seventy acres to tend, there was finally plenty to keep her "workaholic husband" happy. The children were thrilled with the trout ponds, space to roam, and numerous outbuildings to explore. The farm even fulfilled a dream of Moira's — she had always loved old character homes and, now, she had one of her very own.

It was a rambling two-storey structure with a field-stone basement and (finally!) a separate bedroom for each of the Pitt children. The kitchen needed some upgrading and the family wanted a bathroom on the second floor, but the renovations were nothing Moira felt unable to handle. A month before moving in, she bought supplies of paint and wallpaper and set out to work.

As she often worked at the house before or after running errands in nearby Duncan, Moira carried work clothes with her. She would change in the vacant living room of the deserted old farm home, and leave her "street clothes" in a heap on the floor. One day — when Moira was the only person for literally miles around — her change of clothing disappeared. In the empty, unfurnished house, the clothes could not have been misplaced. It was Moira's first clue that when she worked there, she was not alone.

The second clue was the walking.

When Moira tended to some task in the basement, she often heard footsteps across the main floor of the house; when she worked on the main floor, they would criss-cross the second storey. When she investigated there, the elusive sounds appeared to come from the attic. At first, they were easily dismissed as the unfamiliar sounds of an old building. But this was a sturdy house, with no creaks in the floors and, soon, Moira found herself making frequent trips upstairs to ask "who's there?" She was never rewarded with an answer.

Soon, others began to hear the presence. On the occasions that Moira took her five-year-old daughter, Jennifer, to the farmhouse, she claimed also to hear the footsteps, and would laugh as if someone was playing a great joke. Displaying somewhat less good humour was the plumber who threatened to leave his job unfinished, unless he was assured human company while he worked. A carpenter who had been contracted by the Pitts mentioned his otherworldly visitor, but claimed not to be disturbed by it.

Moira, also, was not terribly bothered by whatever it was that roamed the house while they renovated. She sensed nothing hostile in the spirit, and assumed it was simply there to fill the void of an empty house.

"I guess I automatically thought that when we moved in, the ghost would move out," Moira later wrote, adding emphatically, "How wrong I was!"

The first night that the Pitt family spent under their new roof, the entity, in his signature fashion, let them know he had no plans of vacating.

"The ghost walked!" Moira wrote, of that long night. "He thumped through the halls and down the stairs only to reverse his steps and then repeat them. Often there was some thudding that seemed to come from the attic room ... In exhaustion, we all took turns asking him, and then begging him, to quiet down, even for awhile, so we could get some sleep. My husband threw a book and hit the wall, but [the ghost] walked."

The family, deciding that something that noisy had to be male, named their spirit Martin. Now they had a name for what kept them awake at night.

Interestingly, although the sleepless nights led to frustration and brief irritability, not one member of the Pitt family was *frightened* by the unseen house guest. Martin was simply there; something to get used to, like a leaky faucet or a creaking eavestrough.

And, according to Moira, they did get used to him. She wrote, "Sometimes at the breakfast table, one of us would announce that Martin had walked last night. The rest would announce that they had slept and hadn't heard him."

And so, life went on. The Pitts cohabitated peacefully with Martin, and only felt the need to mention his activities if they were having house guests who might be alarmed by him. But, although it was some time before Martin did anything worthy of discussion, it did eventually happen.

Moira was in the kitchen, one afternoon, having coffee with a friend, when there was a loud thump in the attic. It was followed by an alarming crash and, after checking to see that their children were still playing safely on the lawn, both women ran up the stairs to investigate. Another crashing noise rattled the window-panes before Moira reached the attic door and yanked at the latch.

It wouldn't budge.

The door had no lock; it was held shut by a simple latch that had always been easy to open, in the past. Now, no matter how hard Moira tugged at the door, it refused to yield.

Overhead, the banging and thumping continued. Moira's friend grew more excited and frightened by the moment. By the time the noises had subsided to a shuffling sound, then ceased, it was late, and the woman had to take her children home. Moira was pleased to have the chance to investigate alone, as she suspected that the other woman's presence may have caused Martin to bar them both from the attic.

It appeared she was correct. When Moira returned to the door at the top of the stairs, it opened easily. In the dingy attic, she found evidence of Martin's tantrum.

When the Pitts moved into the farmhouse, they had discovered a locked trunk in the attic. Assuming it to be property of the previous owners, they left it alone. After all, the trunk wasn't in the way, and Moira thought someone might return for it, someday.

Now, it looked as though someone had.

The locked trunk was now wide open and resting on the opposite side of the room from where it had been stored. Its contents were strewn wildly across the floor; bits of cloth and paper and a faded collection of old greeting cards and postcards. This scattered collection of mementos obviously meant something to Martin and, as she surveyed the room, Moira resolved to find out who their walking spirit may have been in life.

She began talking to neighbours in the community, and a vague history of the house began to come together. The last people to live there had been a large, close-knit Dutch family, and it was in their folds that Moira believed she found her restless ghost.

The family had a seventeen-year-old son named Albert. One sad Christmas day, a pickup truck that Albert was driving slid terribly out of control and crashed violently into a power pole. Albert had been killed, instantly. When Moira heard the story, she sensed strongly that this was the spirit who endlessly walked the halls of her home.

"I relayed the story to my family," Moira wrote, "and they agreed that perhaps we would get more results if we used the son's name, rather than 'Martin.' Martin became Albert, and Albert was no more quiet than Martin had been. Now, it was Albert that walked and fascinated us."

The Pitt family had been living with Albert for eighteen months when Moira and her husband made plans to take a much-needed vacation. Friends who were familiar with Albert, and not frightened by his presence, agreed to stay at the house and take care of the children. It seemed to be a good plan, but what no one considered was the fact that while the friends were aware of Albert, they were not *accustomed* to him.

Late at night, while the Pitt children slept soundly to the comforting, familiar sounds of Albert's roaming, their caretakers lay awake and exhausted. Night after sleepless night, Albert walked until, finally, the wife could take no more. The weary woman began her own search — for the restless ghost.

In the darkness of the early morning hours she began wandering through the house, looking for Albert, hoping to talk to him. In the downstairs hall she finally sensed the lonely spirit's presence, and began to plead her case.

She was very tired, she explained to him, and thought that since he had been searching so long, he must be worn out as well. She told Albert that his family had moved away, and that he should either join them, or return to the place he had come from. Kindly, she added that while everyone agreed he was a kind and welcome spirit, it was now time for him to rest.

As the woman talked to Albert, his pacing became more agitated. It grew louder and was accompanied by a hollow, thumping sound, as if he dragged some burden behind him. The commotion continued until dawn — and then stopped, forever.

Albert was gone.

When Moira and her husband returned to the farmhouse, they sensed the loss. Although they were met by their own five children, their friends, and the friends' children, Moira described the event as "coming home to an empty house."

The friend who convinced Albert to leave likely thought she was doing the Pitts a great favour, but, in reality, the boy's presence was sorely missed. His nocturnal walks had lulled the family to sleep for so long, the absence of them resulted in tossing and turning. After many restless hours, Moira discovered that if she left a radio on in the house, it helped everyone to sleep.

Later, when writing about Albert, Moira noted sadly, "He never returned. We called the family of Albert and asked them about the trunk. I think someone finally came and picked it up.

"The house, strangely empty, was finally ours."

And, hopefully, Albert, who had walked for so long, found a place, somewhere, that he could finally call home.

An Unwelcome Premonition

Moira Pitt's gift of receiving messages through her psychic abilities has not always been a welcome, or even helpful, one. On several occasions she has been privy to terrible knowledge of events that she was powerless to change. The worst of these events involved one of her own children.

"In early September of 1980, as I exited from the mud room in our ranch home in northeastern BC to the carport," she later wrote, "I heard the message, 'You are going to lose one of your children!'"

As Moira leaned, shaking and weak-kneed, against her Ford Bronco, the names of her children were presented to her, as if on a wide, white screen. First, "Kerry," Moira's oldest son, who was married and living away from home. The answer on the screen was "no." Then, "Blaise," the second-oldest, who had recently been accepted into the RCMP and was waiting for his assignment in Regina. Again, the answer was "no." Then, "Jamie." Moira felt frozen to the spot; numb with grief and pain as the devastating reply came: "yes."

Jamie was Moira's third son; nineteen years old and still living at home. He worked in the oil patch and had just made arrangements to take courses that would complete his grade twelve. He hoped to join the RCMP, as his older brother had. Moira described his zest for life, saying, "He lived it in double time. Always a smile and a laugh, always lots of friends of all ages ..."

And now Moira was being told that her son would be taken from her.

"Why do I have to know this?" she cried, anger now mingling with the grief.

"So you can be prepared," was the cryptic reply. As if anyone could prepare for the death of a child.

For weeks, Moira carried the burden of this terrible information alone. She considered telling her husband, or a friend, but knew that she would only be causing them pain. She thought about warning Jamie, but felt he could do nothing to change what was inevitable. "What could he do?" she thought. "Hide? Stop living? Live in fear?"

In the end, Moira told no one. And she hoped and prayed that the message was wrong.

A frightening series of close calls and accidents befell Jamie through the month of September, and Moira almost began to relax. As the weeks went by, she thought that perhaps her son was fated to experience a string of bad luck, but survive it all. Sadly, she was wrong.

Moira Pitt holds a portrait of her son Jamie, who was murdered on October 9, 1980. Weeks before, Moira was given the terrifying message that she would lose him.
(Photograph by Jean Roux, Osoyoos; courtesy of Moira Pitt)

One Wednesday evening in early October, Jamie went into town to have a drink with a friend. He promised to be home around midnight. Moira waved goodbye at the front door, unaware that it was the last time she would see her son alive.

Later, Moira would write, "What do I say? For all the warning I had, I slept through his [death]. While I slept, my son died."

In the October 14, 1980 issue of the *Province*, a small article began as follows:

> DAWSON CREEK — A 16-year-old youth was charged Monday with two counts of murder following a police investigation of two shooting deaths during the last five days.

One of the murder victims was James Barron Pitt — Moira's beloved "Jamie." He had been killed not more than a mile from his home by a juvenile who wanted his car. Apparently, the sixteen-year-old was on the run, having committed another murder earlier in the evening. Jamie had kindly agreed to give the youth a ride ten miles up the Alaska highway, unaware that he was making a fatal mistake.

It was a simple action that fulfilled Moira's terrible premonition.

Nearly one year to the day after Jamie's death, Moira's second-oldest son, Gordon Blaise Pitt, graduated from the RCMP academy in Regina.

"This graduation is for two," Moira said to herself, as she sat and watched the ceremonies. No sooner had she completed that thought, when Blaise rose to receive his badge — and as he walked to the awards area, a shadowy figure appeared to walk beside him. When Blaise stood proudly on the stage, he did not stand alone. When Moira wiped away her tears, she could plainly see the figure of James Barron Pitt at his side.

"It is my belief," Moira later wrote, "that the ones we love are never far away. Jamie is still there for us all."

And that's a bit of otherworldly knowledge she doesn't mind being privy to.

An Impatient Presence

By 1990, Moira Pitt's older children had grown and moved away. Only Jennifer, the youngest, still lived with her parents when they decided to relocate to the south Okanagan.

Together in the realtor's office, the family pored over photographs of houses and property. "For once," Moira noted, "my poor husband would have liked something newer that didn't require work." But it wasn't meant to be.

Jennifer was immediately taken with a picture of a Dutch Colonial farmhouse, surrounded by lush greenery and rolling hills. Moira tried to take a practical approach, thinking of all the work the run-down property required, but her love of charming old homes won out. As for Moira's husband, she said, "The two women in his life just overruled him and carried on."

The house, grounds, and orchard had been neglected over recent years, and a general restoration was in order. Moira's husband set out to restore the orchard to its former glory. Jennifer cleaned all the out-buildings, scrubbing the floors with oil soap until they gleamed, then set up a tack room and grooming station for her beloved horses. Moira, herself, began dealing with the wild condition of the flower beds outside and, inside, tried to brighten the old house with fresh paint and wallpaper.

Shortly after buying the house, the family heard the first disembodied footsteps. Moira, recalling their experience in the mid-1970s, thought, "Here we go again." But, as it turned out, this was to be a different haunting experience for the Pitts.

At that time, Jennifer was an equestrian coach, and the bulk of her work fell on weekends and after school hours. This left her alone in the house for most of the day and, therefore, she was the first to really become acquainted with the spirit.

"She said that there was a little dog with the ghost," explained Moira, adding that Jennifer's own constant companion

As they refurbished this property in the south Okanagan, the Pitt family was visited by a spirit who constantly urged them to "Hurry, hurry!"

(Photograph courtesy of Moira Pitt)

was a small red Cocker Spaniel named Casey. On several occasions, Jennifer was certain she heard Casey barking in another part of the house when, in fact, the little dog was right by her feet.

One day, as Moira walked up the stairs, she felt something brush past her. Startled, she stopped, and could clearly hear the scampering footsteps of a small dog. "There was nothing to be seen!" Moira exclaimed. She had just met the little spirit dog, and would soon become acquainted with its master.

Moira was hard at work, painting a spare bedroom, one evening, when she experienced a strong sense of someone standing behind her. Several times she turned, expecting to see her husband or daughter standing there. Each time, she found the room empty. Finally, over her shoulder, she distinctly heard the words, "Hurry, hurry!" Again, she spun around, but found no one to go with the mysterious voice.

After that, Moira often felt she was being watched, as she worked in the house or around the yard. Frequently, the strange, phantom voice urged her to "Hurry, hurry!" Moira felt she was being encouraged to complete her restoration of the farm and house; indeed, all three members of the Pitt family felt nearly driven to do so.

Considering the ghost's apparent mission, Moira wondered if he might be the spirit of the man who had built the home and homesteaded the property. The man had lived there for more than fifty years, and created one of the Okanagan's most richly productive organic farms. Surely, he had despaired to see the place fall into disrepair over the years — and would be anxious to see it refurbished. The Pitts considerately tried to ease the ghost's mind by talking out loud, while they worked, of their plans for the farm. Still, they were constantly urged to "Hurry, hurry!" And occasionally, they were puzzled by the scurrying sound of a small dog on the staircase.

The dog might have remained a mystery, but Moira explained, "One day, a nephew of the former owner dropped by the house. We stood talking in the kitchen as Casey, our Cocker Spaniel, came into the kitchen and exited through the dining room. The nephew paled and asked if he had really seen a little dog walk through the kitchen. We told him that that was our daughter's Cocker [Spaniel]. 'Thank goodness,' he said. 'My uncle had one just like that, and he called it Casey. I thought I was seeing a ghost!'"

Amazed at the coincidence, Moira told the man that their dog was *also* named Casey. Then, cautiously, she went on to explain that there did seem to be a ghost on the premises — and that she felt it might be his uncle.

"He didn't laugh," Moira said. "He told us that his uncle had loved the farm and, if anyone would come back to see to the restoration, his uncle would."

In fact, it seemed as though it was the old man's only reason for haunting his former home, for once the land and house were returned to their original state, he seemed to slip away. His disappearance was gradual; the Pitts just eventually realized that they hadn't been visited by the ghost or his little four-legged companion for some time.

"The farm thrived and converted to organic, once again, with very little trouble," Moira wrote. "We were often told it was one of the most trouble-free organic farms in the valley. We are sure the old man still looked after it while we slept, but we never saw or felt him or his dog again."

*****

After many decades of receiving premonitory messages and experiencing contact with the spirit world, Moira Pitt has finally come to accept her gift.

"It took a long time for me to realize that I was a sensitive," she admits, adding that she now trusts the messages she is given, and is working as a psychic. Using tarot cards and various other methods, Moira reads professionally under the name "Tory." That, and her freelance writing career, absorbs most of her time.

"I laughingly say I am retired but, in truth, retirement is ten years away," she says.

For a woman who is predestined to experience the extraordinary, ten years should bring another lifetime of excitement.

CHAPTER THREE

The Haunted Hotels

If there is one commonly accepted theory among the disparate views of paranormal theorists, it would be that wherever there have been people, there are ghosts.

With that in mind, British Columbia's countless hotels and motels make natural habitats for the province's earth-bound spirits. They see a steady and diverse flow of human traffic. Dramas ranging from weddings to deaths are played out daily. The older hotels (including the Jones Hotel, now the Black Nugget Museum mentioned in chapter 1) have often played significant roles in a larger historical picture.

All that activity must ensure a healthy afterlife. As the following stories clearly show, in BC's haunted hotels, there are some guests who never leave.

Rights of a Ghost: The Harbour House Hotel Story

"Do spirits have rights?"

That was the question asked in the headline of a front page article in the January 25, 1995 edition of the *Gulf Islands Driftwood*. The answer, according to psychic Alexei Rainier, who was quoted in the body of the article, is that they do.

It's easy to wonder why this strange issue would crop up in a weekly newspaper published in the sleepy little town of Ganges, on Salt Spring Island. But the reason was simple: the rights of phantoms had become a hot topic for a local business, the Harbour House Hotel.

The Harbour House Hotel, on Ganges Harbour, advertises "hospitality the way it's supposed to be." In a glossy full-colour hand-out, you can read about the "clean ocean-front rooms," "large balconies," and "full facilities for every occasion." But what the hotel chooses to omit from its public image is what is undeniably most interesting: the Harbour House is haunted.

The story, and the haunting, began in 1973 with the murder of a man named Walter Herzog. Walter was the owner of the Harbour House — he had purchased the property in 1971, planning to transform the hotel into a renowned resort.

Walter was a man of action. Within a year, he had added a wing to the existing building. In the fall of 1972, the hotel burned to the ground. Undaunted, Walter rebuilt. In September of 1973, he was planning a grand reopening celebration when fate dealt the ultimate blow.

In the early morning hours of September 15, 1973, Walter Herzog apparently confronted a burglar in his private suite. A few hours later, a hotel staff member discovered his body; five bullets had been pumped into his chest and stomach.

Walter was dead and, coincidently, since that day, the Harbour House Hotel has always seemed to host one extra, unregistered, invisible guest.

*****

A psychic, who visited the Harbour House nearly twenty years after the murder, announced to the staff that she sensed a ghost in the hotel. She even offered a type of diagnostic proof: an onion, quartered and left in the four corners of the pub, became rotted and slimy overnight. The psychic said that the accelerated deterioration of the onion proved the presence of a ghost. The staff agreed, but the test had really been unnecessary. People at the Harbour House Hotel had been experiencing strange phenomena for two decades. They had their own proof.

There were the noises; sounds of sweeping, rolling marbles, and the disturbing effect of something heavy being dragged across the floor. It would always happen in the early hours of the morning, between one-thirty and six, and no cause was ever discovered.

On a stroll through the hotel, people would often encounter columns of inexplicably cold air, or what they would describe as a "thickening" of the air and the sense of a presence, although they appeared to be alone.

Much of the activity has taken place in the pub, which was once the location of Walter Herzog's private suite, and in the rooms directly above and below it. The room below is used to house the bands that come to play at the hotel.

"We've decided he doesn't like bands at all," manager, Ann Ringheim, is quoted as saying in the *Gulf Islands Driftwood*. The result is that bands don't like Walter, either. After being subjected to eerie moaning sounds, whispery conversations of disembodied voices, and other strange happenings, there are many musicians who now elect to sleep in their vans instead of taking advantage of the free accommodations.

The hotel staff, perhaps being so accustomed to Walter's presence, is much less disturbed by it. Ann Ringheim, herself, has grown very used to the activity since becoming manager. The fact that none of the ghostly goings-on seem threatening probably helps.

"He just plays little pranks to let you know he's around," Ann told Valorie Lennox of the *Driftwood*, explaining that she sees Walter as a "friendly ghost."

Friendly? Perhaps. But definitely disruptive.

The pinball machine in the pub sometimes plays on its own for up to thirty minutes. The jukebox can be turned off — even unplugged — yet compact discs begin flipping over on their own. In the men's washroom, turning on one water faucet occasionally prompts two others to follow suit — even though all three taps have separate pipes. Calculators switch on, without being touched, and spit out lists of numbers. During closing time, as the staff prepares to leave, one beer tap will suddenly flip open. And after closing time, when the stereo, lights, and television have been turned off, and the doors to the pub locked, the TV often comes back on at full volume.

Ann Ringheim is willing to concede that "We do get a lot of power surges on the island ... but when something is *unplugged*, that just doesn't explain it."

One of Walter's unexplainable tricks has been a particular source of frustration for Ann. It seems that he likes to play with telephones. The article in the *Gulf Islands Driftwood* explained:

> Staff began receiving calls from room 206 on the switchboard. No one was ever on the line and the calls only occurred when the room was empty.
>
> The incidents became annoying, so both phone boxes in the room were disconnected and the phone removed.
>
> But the phone kept registering on the switchboard. Now the calls were directed to the rooms of other guests, ringing at two or three a.m. Sometimes, the dialling continued all night, prompting a storm of complaints from guests.

"I've had BC Tel in three times and they can't figure out what's wrong with the phones," Ringheim said.

Perhaps it's something to do with the fact that room 206 is situated directly above Walter Herzog's murder site.

*****

Despite all of the manifestations of the ghost that is believed to have been Walter Herzog, Ann Ringheim has yet to be frightened. In fact, her reaction is quite the contrary.

"After awhile it's almost comforting ... all these silly little things that happen. You go, 'oh, he's around.'" To Valorie Lennox of the *Gulf Islands Driftwood*, she described it as "a real neat feeling. Walter's always looking after you."

What's more, Ann believes that the situation is agreeable to Walter, as well. She believes he is content to remain in his beloved hotel, playing jokes on the staff.

Alexei Rainier believes quite differently and, so, the debate — over the rights of a ghost — begins.

Rainier, a White Rock psychic and ordained Spiritualist Church minister, believes that Walter Herzog is being exploited. When she offered to exorcise his spirit from the Harbour House and was declined, she spoke out against manager Ann Ringheim in the *Gulf Islands Driftwood*. "She [the manager] wants to keep Walter because that makes the hotel interesting," was her accusing quote.

According to Rainier, she had visited the haunted hotel, and felt a very strong sense of "turmoil and imbalance" caused by Herzog's trapped, confused spirit. She also believes that with the passing of time, and an accumulation of frustration, Walter's spirit will become more tormented and dangerous to deal with. "He could start to create disturbances throughout the hotel you couldn't believe," she warned in the *Driftwood*.

Ann Ringheim isn't frightened by this prospect; she believes Walter is happy to be where he is. However, she did think it appropriate to consider the ghost's own opinion. After meeting Alexei Rainier, she asked Walter for a sign if he wished to remain in the hotel. The next morning, she received one; a series of numbers on the display of the switchboard, which had inexplicably gone off-line, overnight.

Ann deciphered the code by matching the numbers to corresponding letters on a telephone pad. The resulting message: "*BOO.*" Ann Ringheim believes the playful message indicates that Walter is enjoying himself, and doesn't want to leave.

Not surprisingly, Alexei Rainier studied the same numbers and interpreted a different message. She believes Walter's answer was "*NO,*" meaning he wants to move on to another plane of existence.

They may disagree on why he is there; they may disagree on whether he wishes to remain there; but people who have experienced the strange phenomena at the Harbour House Hotel never disagree that Walter Herzog *is* there. And there he shall remain — either happily in residence or sadly trapped — until the rights and privileges owed his spirit can be agreed upon.

"We Call It 'Casper'"

A few years ago, if you had asked Anneke Leupin if she believed in ghosts, she likely would have told you "no." Since then, she has become the owner and operator of a roadside motel in Williams Lake and her opinion on the paranormal has changed.

In March of 1995, Anneke wrote, "I bought this motel about six years ago and have enjoyed running it with my staff ... we have worked together, the same group, since I got this place."

The group she speaks of includes four women: Colleen, Charlotte, Johanna, and Elaine. They were all well-known, trusted employees; so when they began to tell Anneke about strange experiences they had in the motel, she was inclined to take them seriously.

They explained that they would be cleaning one particular room when, suddenly, the television would loudly come to life on its own. In that same room, they would be busy making the beds when the faucet in the unoccupied bathroom would begin to gush. On one occasion, two of the women witnessed an ashtray shaking violently about on a very stable tabletop. Two other times, they ventured down to the supply room to pick up some clothes hangers for the mysteriously empty closets, only to return moments later and find the rods jangling with hangers.

"When the girls are on their coffee break in the laundry room they distinctly hear footsteps upstairs, and even whistling," Anneke elaborated. She knew this first-hand, having heard the footsteps herself. Still, she found it hard to believe that their quiet motel had a supernatural guest. That belief was to change.

"Last night made me change my mind," Anneke wrote in her letter. "I was in the basement, planting my seedling ... alone, or so I thought. Suddenly I felt hands running up and down my waist area. I, of course, jumped and turned to see who was there, and I saw no one." Frightened, Anneke finished her planting elsewhere.

Although such unexpected visits can be unsettling, Anneke Leupin and her staff don't believe their spirit means anyone harm. In fact, "We call it 'Casper,' because it's friendly," was her comment on that.

Apparently, no one minds if Casper never checks out of this comfortable motel in Williams Lake.

A Spirit Summons

Roughly thirty miles from the Yukon border sits the northern BC community of Atlin. For many years, one of the landmark sites was the Kootenay Hotel; a structure that Atlinites must have felt was a necessity, as they gathered together to rebuild it twice — each time after fires that devastated the town.

Fortunately, the third Kootenay Hotel proved more enduring. It was built in 1917, after the second fire, and was destined to stand for decades to come. Eventually, it would become home to an Atlin ghost.

Diane S. Smith of the Atlin Historical Society first heard the story in the late fall of 1968, when she and her husband became the new owners of the Kootenay Hotel.

"At one time, the Indians from the Telegraph area were taken to Whitehorse for medical treatment," she wrote. "Usually, they were flown to Atlin in one of the bush planes and then probably driven the rest of the way on the mail bus. They had to [stay] overnight here, and they stayed at the Kootenay Hotel."

Two fires down; one to go. Atlinites stand proudly in front of the Kootenay Hotel in 1917, shortly after it was rebuilt for the second time.
(Photograph courtesy of the Atlin Historical Society)

Apparently, one regular traveller was an elderly native woman who loved to smoke, but could not be trusted with her own matches. The proprietor of the hotel at that time offered a thoughtful solution: she was always booked into room 11, directly above the office. When the old lady wanted a cigarette, she simply tapped on the floor with her cane and the proprietor, upon hearing the signal below, would come upstairs and give her a light.

One night, the man was busy, and took a little longer than usual to answer the woman's signal. When he opened the door to room 11, he found her dead, cane in hand.

"After that happened," Diane explained, "a tapping sound was often heard coming from room 11 or nearby. I never heard it, but one of my staff claimed she did. A telephone company man who occupied the room across the hall for a period of time told us he had heard it at the same time, each night."

Over the years, several people made frustrating attempts to find a logical explanation for the tapping. One woman crawled on hands and knees through every inch of the attic, looking for anything that might have been bumping or scraping together. Another time, the entire exterior of the hotel was examined for wires, loose siding, or anything that might move rhythmically in the wind. No explanation for the tapping in room 11 was ever found.

As for Diane Smith, she saw no need to rid the Kootenay of its unusual phenomenon. "I certainly didn't mind sharing the hotel with a ghostly guest," she claims. "She didn't take up any space, and most people who used room 11 never heard her. [Also], no one ever saw her."

And now, no one ever will. In late November of 1969, just one year after Diane and her husband bought the Kootenay Hotel, it burned to the ground. At this one location in Atlin, there had been three Kootenay Hotels and three horrible fires. This time, no one had the heart to rebuild.

As for the old woman's ghost, Diane claims, "As far as I know, she has not been heard from again. Maybe she just went home to Telegraph Creek."

Or, maybe she was satisfied that someone finally brought her a light.

Whistler's Mocking Ghosts

In the early eighties, it was the "Creekhouse"; a pub and lodge built to meet the needs of Whistler's flourishing tourist trade. Today, it has split into two separate entities — Whistler Creek Lodge and Serrebello Restaurant — but something of the past still unites them: ghosts.

In the restaurant, "There are two ghosts, one is a mother and the other is a child, possibly about twelve years old." The quote comes from an article written by Doug Alexander in the October 27, 1994 edition of *The Whistler Question*. These apparitions have been seen, by numerous diners and staff members, sitting up in the rafters of the restaurant. If that seems strange, the ghostly pair's behaviour is even more puzzling; they are always witnessed peering down at the Serrebello patrons and laughing uproariously.

In Alexander's article, former general manager Robert Seguin spoke of his experiences at the restaurant. "I never saw the ghosts, but strange things seemed to happen up there. Lights went off and things would move up on the shelves near the rafters."

Seguin claims to have been a sceptic, originally, but changed his attitude after witnessing some eerie events and hearing identical stories from a variety of sources.

In the lodge, connected to the restaurant, there have also been several witnesses to a presence that wanders the hallways. The difference: this particular ghost isn't laughing. One woman who encountered the sinister spook relayed the experience to Doug Alexander. He described it in *The Whistler Question*:

> The woman felt the ghost was disturbed and she
> had a bad feeling about this supernatural presence.
> Terrified from the evil impression, she vowed to
> never again search for that ghost.

Frightening or fun-loving, the tourists and residents have their choice of paranormal types in this connected lodge and restaurant, in the town of Whistler.

Haunting at the Heriot Bay Inn

According to locals, there is a legend that goes as follows:

In the early days of this century, a logger with a little time off decided to visit the Heriot Bay Inn on Quadra Island. The Inn, built just years earlier, in 1894, was a popular spot. The logger was looking forward to a little social activity. What he got was a fight.

A brawl between the logger and some other men broke out inside the hotel. Eventually, the ruckus moved outside, where the logger paid for the confrontation with his life. The man's assailants buried his body in a triangular lot across from the Inn and hoped that would be the end of it. The logger, however, found no peace, and continues to wander through the hotel where he had hoped to spend some pleasant time off.

This is a bit of Quadra Island's folklore, handed down over generations. It would be difficult, if not impossible, to confirm the story of the unfortunate logger's murder, yet many people believe it to be true. Of course, lending credibility to this story is the fact that something supernatural does, indeed, seem to wander through the century-old structure still known as the Heriot Bay Inn.

Tanya Storr is a writer and photographer from nearby Quathiaski Cove. Her interest in the subject of ghosts inspired her to collect stories from some of the people who had experienced strange things at the Heriot Bay Inn. The tales she heard were compelling. The attitudes she encountered were of equal interest.

"Many former rationalists who say they never used to believe in the supernatural have changed their tune after encounters with uncanny phenomena at the Inn," she wrote. It seems that seeing is believing; and what follows are first-hand

The Heriot Bay Inn, in 1911.
(Photograph courtesy of Campbell River Museum and Archives; catalogue #7676)

The Heriot Bay Inn, in 1995. Many decades have passed, and many changes have been made, but the same ghost still roams this building.

(Photograph courtesy of Tanya Storr)

accounts, from Tanya's files, of what three people saw at the Heriot Bay Inn.

*****

A female bartender, who worked at the Heriot Bay Inn for seven years, had an eerie encounter in the pub, one day.

"It was early fall in 1987; one of those autumn days when the sun was shining and the leaves were orange. It was a humdrum, dead day and no one had been in, yet, for a drink.

"I was standing on a stool, stocking the beer fridge, with my back to the front door. I heard the front door open ... felt the draft ... felt someone standing there looking at me ... and then I heard the door swing shut. I didn't want to turn around right away, because I didn't want to drop any of the bottles.

"As my customer approached the bar, I heard the shuffling sound of two pant-legs rubbing together, and out of my peripheral vision, I saw a tall skinny man standing there. He had short dark hair and was wearing clothes like the ones the loggers are wearing in the old black and white photographs in the pub; durable and heavy, but worn. I didn't think much of the man's outfit at the time, though. All I was thinking was, 'Alright! My first customer!', and I was glad he was waiting patiently, while I unloaded the last of my bottles.

"I then turned around to say, 'Can I get you something to drink?', but the words died on my lips ... for there was *nobody* there at all."

*****

One man who managed the Heriot Bay Inn had an unnerving and unexplainable experience there in the late 1980s. It was the Inn's quiet winter season, when it happened.

"I was living in the Heriot Bay Inn, in the apartment that overlooks the bay. One night, when I was the only one there, I heard a loud racket outside. It must've been two o'clock in the morning, at least, because the pub was closed, all the lights were off in the building, and everything was locked up.

"I thought it was a bunch of dogs getting into the garbage containers ... eventually I got tired of the noise and went downstairs to scare them away.

"I went out the front doors, locking them behind me, and grabbed a couple of rocks to throw at the dogs. But once I got outside, everything was strangely quiet. I walked around the campground, but there were no dogs out there ... there was nothing around.

"Then I turned back to look at the Inn, and got the shock of my life when I saw that every light on the main floor was blazing, although they had all been off when I went outside just a few minutes before. The second floor was still dark; just all the lights on the first floor were on.

"I hurried back to the Inn, only to find everything still locked. I then went through the building, thinking somebody must have found a way in, but there was nobody there. There were no people or dogs around at all, to explain either the cause of the noises or the lights.

"The whole thing was pretty spooky."

*****

One winter, a local man rented a room at the Heriot Bay Inn for one month. It being the off-season, he was the only guest, and had a perfect opportunity to acquaint himself with some of the hotel's more unusual attractions.

"Many times I was in my room upstairs on nights when I was alone at the hotel, and I could actually hear somebody coming down the hall. I'd just lay there quietly, waiting for a door to open, but I wouldn't hear anything else.

"A couple of times, I opened my door up and looked down the hall, and there wouldn't be a damn soul in the hallway. But I'd know I'd just heard someone walking down the hall! A hundred and one things would go around in my head, like, 'Maybe it's just the building settling.' But it wasn't the building settling; it happened too many times to be that.

"One night the manager, another guy who worked at the Inn, and I were sitting in the manager's apartment watching movies. We were the only people in the place and the building was all locked up.

"As we were sitting there, we heard footsteps come down the hall, go down the stairs, and into the pub area. We all looked at one another as if to say, 'Who the hell is in the building?' We figured anyone who was in there must have busted into the place, so we all charged out, expecting to catch somebody on the main floor.

"We were determined to catch this person, and it didn't take us a minute to get from our asses, to our feet, to the door, to downstairs. Not enough time passed for someone to unlock the front doors and get out that way, so we assumed the intruder went through the tackle shop into the kitchen or the pub ... We split up; [they] went into the kitchen, and I went into the front hallway and then through the tackle shop and into the bar that way.

"We thought that maybe the person was hiding under the pool tables, so we checked the whole damn place out, checked the washrooms, checked everywhere — and there wasn't a soul there! But the three of us had distinctly heard somebody walk down those stairs ... and we all just stood there in the pub with egg on our faces, saying, 'Okay, we all heard it, but who was it?'"

*****

According to Tanya Storr, these three accounts are a mere sampling of the many stories she has collected about the Heriot Bay Inn.

Could it be the murdered logger causing so much activity? No one knows, but clearly, something unexplainable lives within those old walls.

CHAPTER FOUR

Destinations: Unknown

Any map of Vancouver Island will provide you with the usual information on cities and towns, highways and byways, names of places, and ways to reach them. What will surely be omitted, however, are some of the Island's more interesting features — networks of gravel and pavement that are lined with alarming sights and sensations, suddenly unfamiliar scenery, and strange shifts in time.

These are Vancouver Island's haunted highways and, for the adventurous traveller, they offer a more unusual trip, by far.

Miss Stiff: The Sooke Spinster

It was just before midnight on a dark, rainy evening in early November. Michel and Marion Des Rochers were driving along East Sooke Road, on their way into Langford, to pick up their son. Rain pelted the pavement, washing the road in reflected light from the 1980 Zephyr's high-beams. It was a miserable night to drive, and most people in this rural area chose not to. The Des Rochers appeared to have the highway to themselves.

Just west of Park Heights Drive, near Anderson Cove, the car rounded a sharp corner. Marion Des Rochers described the moment to reporter Patrick Murphy in the November 26, 1989 edition of the Victoria *Times-Colonist*.

> It was dark and raining ... We were rounding the corner ... You have to keep to the right. Suddenly we came across this figure at the yellow line on the left side.
>
> She was dressed in Edwardian clothing; a long dress and wide hat. I had the impression she had [button up] boots on.

The Des Rochers' vehicle passed so close by this careless pedestrian, Marion later claimed that, had she opened her window, she could have touched her. The shock of having so very nearly hit the woman froze her appearance into memory.

"She had a very pale, grey face," Marion Des Rochers told the *Times-Colonist*. "She was not looking at us; it was like she was looking through us." Marion recalled the woman looking very sad, and having quite a homely appearance. She seemed unfazed by her close call, and remained standing by the centre line on the highway, even after the car hurtled past. As Marion Des Rochers touched her brakes, briefly, and saw the strange, calm woman silhouetted in the red lights, she realized what had been most remarkable about her appearance.

She wasn't wet.

It was unusual, but forgettable, at the time. The Des Rochers drove on, slightly shaken and quite angry over the irresponsibility of certain pedestrians. It was not until days later, when they shared the story with a neighbour, that another possibility occurred to them.

The neighbour dismissed the story with a single sentence. She said that Michel and Marion must have seen the school teacher's ghost.

The suggestion that their experience had been supernatural made the Des Rochers give it some more thought. They agreed that it had been out of the ordinary, so Marion decided to phone the local museum to find out if there had once been a school in East Sooke. What she found out was much, much more.

According to Elida Peers, of the Sooke Region Museum, the couple's strange, late-night experience was not a unique one. It seems that several residents of Sooke and East Sooke had witnessed a similar apparition by that particular bend in the road. Some had been alarmed enough to make a report to the local RCMP. Others, as did the Des Rochers, inquired timidly at the local museum. But all came to a common conclusion: the pale woman who stood sadly in the middle of East Sooke Road had been dead since before the Great Depression. What people were seeing was a ghost — the spirit of a schoolteacher named Louisa Mary Stiff.

Miss Stiff was one of East Sooke's first teachers; a spinster who lived in the area and, eventually, died of cancer in a Victoria hospital when she was still in her fifties. What may connect her to the oft-seen apparition is the report that Miss Stiff once suffered a bad fall when she was thrown from a buggy on the very turn of the road that now appears to be haunted.

If pictures of the young school-marm exist, she may also have been identified by witnesses to the ghost — although descriptions of the spirit vary interestingly.

A man named Calvin Reichelt told the museum's Elida Peers about seeing the famous lady standing on the road at high noon one misty day. He stopped to offer her a ride, then gawked in disbelief as she ignored him and walked directly through the front of his car. His account was recorded in the *Times-Colonist*:

> She was different altogether from the other descriptions. She was about 25 and good-looking. I know because I saw her as close as I can see my hand as she walked through the motor compartment.

Besides witnessing a younger, more attractive woman, Calvin Reichelt noted that his apparition was wearing a long, white gown — not the dark clothing she was seen in at night.

Another person who claimed to see Miss Stiff in the rain and fog early one morning reported another discrepancy: the ghost who is always seen as being unusually dry in very rainy conditions was, this time, soaking wet.

Calvin Reichelt offered his explanation in the *Times-Colonist*, saying, "It must be ... she can change her appearance for different people." No matter what the woman looked like, though, his conclusion remains the same: "I know it was a ghost."

Shortly after the Des Rochers met the lonely ghost on that wet, dark night, the *Sooke Mirror* ran a story about the spooky sightings. In response, a niece of Louisa Mary Stiff wrote a letter to the editor, recalling memories of the woman she called "Aunt Lulie."

The niece challenged the many reports of Miss Stiff's homely face, asserting that she had been a thin woman, "but quite attractive." She described her beloved aunt as a gentlewoman in every way, and wrote that "She would be the last person to want to become the subject of a romanticized myth."

That's a shame — because in life, Louisa Mary Stiff was remembered mainly as a rather plain schoolteacher. In death, she now has become a legendary part of local folklore; the mysterious "Sooke Spinster."

A Time-Shift on Shelbourne Street

Hauntings usually seem to be a human connection between the past and the present, but there are indications that some *places* are able to make those connections on their own. In the cool, fall weeks of October leading up to Hallowe'en, one street in Victoria is said to make such a "haunting" connection — by presenting a visual memory of the dirt-packed country road that it once was.

Witnesses to the eerie transformation are usually alone in their vehicles, between two and three o'clock on a Sunday morning. As they drive along Shelbourne Street, south of the Hillside shopping centre, they become convinced they've taken a wrong turn.

The confusion is understandable, for the ordinary city street lined with streetlights, houses, and shops has unexpectedly become an overgrown country road. Wild grass grows up between the tire ruts, and flowering broom and bulrushes bunch thickly together in the marshy ditches. The dirt road is deserted and dark, but just as the lone traveller begins searching desperately for a place to make a U-turn, the bright lights of Hillside are suddenly all around.

Have people seen the "ghost" of what Shelbourne Street once was, or have they momentarily travelled back to that time? It's a rare and fascinating phenomenon that occurs each October in Victoria's early morning hours.

A Soldier's Last Moments

In their book *A Gathering of Ghosts* (1989), authors Robin Skelton and Jean Kozocari write about a roadside apparition that has been seen since the Second World War.

"Just past Christie Point," they write, "under a railway trestle, the highway curves gently as it begins to climb a small hill. On the left, about halfway up the hill, is a small pub."

Apparently, for more than five decades, night-time motorists on this stretch of road have witnessed the agonizing last moments of a young soldier's life.

It always begins when people slam on their brakes to avoid hitting what appears to be a large dog. Once they've stopped, however, and the figure is clearly seen in the glare of headlights, people are shocked to see that it is a man in a long khaki army coat. He crawls slowly along on hands and knees, his black hair falling forward, hiding his face. The soldier appears to be in great pain, but when drivers jump out of their cars to assist him, the apparition simply fades away.

"Had he been beaten and was he crawling to the pub for help? Or was the poor soldier so inebriated that he couldn't walk?" Skelton and Kozocari speculate. "As he is always seen by people in cars," they conclude, "it is likely that he was the victim of a car accident."

If ever you drive by this small pub on the hill past Christie Point, be watching for this sad soldier who's relived his painful death on the roadside for more than half a century.

The Chinese Hitchhiker

Several years ago in Victoria, a radio talk-show host was examining the subject of local ghost stories. One of his listeners phoned in to tell an unsettling tale of an experience she had shared with her husband on a stretch of road between Victoria and Sooke that is locally known as "China Flats." Before the woman was even able to finish her eerie account, the radio station's switchboard lit up with calls. It seemed many people who had driven that road came away with a similarly strange story to tell.

Frequently, people driving along the China Flats road will see a shadowy figure leap out of the ditch, directly in front of their vehicle. Drivers always swerve wildly and slam on their brakes; but when they've come to a full stop and can go back to investigate, they never find anyone or anything to explain what they saw.

Other travellers suddenly feel that something powerful and unseen has joined them in their vehicle. The sensation is usually so strong, people are afraid to turn around and check the back seat. When two people are riding together, the overwhelming fear and feeling of being watched strikes both at the same time. And usually, just as suddenly as when it starts, the sensation will disappear.

Person after person called the talk show, that day, claiming to have witnessed this bizarre phenomenon, but no one could explain what the cause of the supernatural disturbance might be. Finally, one long-time resident of the area shared this tale.

Apparently, in the early 1940s, there was a Chinese couple who farmed the land that lies close to that stretch of road. One night, the wife became very ill, and the husband ran to find help. His hope was to hitch a ride to the nearest town and bring back a doctor to help his wife, but the task proved more difficult than he thought.

People must have been too wary to stop for a stranger on a dark night, as car after car sped past him. Finally, in one last desperate attempt to save his wife, the man stepped directly in front of a vehicle and began waving his arms. Either the driver didn't see him, or was unable to stop, for the poor farmer was struck down and killed.

This was a compound tragedy. When the police officers who investigated the accident went to the farmhouse to deliver the terrible news to the man's wife, they found that she, also, had died, for want of medical attention.

Perhaps her husband thinks she is still in need of a doctor, and is still trying frantically to find some help. Or perhaps he haunts the road as revenge against the many motorists who refused to stop for him.

Whatever the reason, many decades later, the Chinese Hitchhiker is still trying to catch a ride.

The Mists of Time

There are those who believe that climate bears great influence on paranormal phenomena, supposedly because ghosts require certain physical conditions before they can appear. The theory is that humidity plays a key role. While it's doubtful that all the fog machines on Hollywood movie sets have been erected in the interest of accuracy, rather than atmosphere, there's no denying the sheer volume of ghost stories that take place on rainy nights, misty mornings, and near bodies of water.

Phyllis Griffiths, a writer from Victoria, opened her fascinating tale of retrocognition (seeing into the past) with a mood-setting description of such weather.

"It was a grey and foggy mid-October afternoon in 1986," she wrote, "when three young teenage boys decided to go on a bicycling trip to nearby Goldstream Provincial Park."

The young fellows in question were Phyllis's sons, Ken and Chris Griffiths, and Mike Waring, a close family friend whom Phyllis regards as a son. The three spent much of their time together and had shared many adventures, but none would compare to the mystery they were destined to experience on that fall afternoon.

The boys pedalled out along the Trans-Canada Highway for a distance, then decided to alter their route to avoid an intimidating hill. They opted to use Sooke Lake Road as a detour and enjoyed a leisurely ride, although the area was littered with pockets of dense fog.

"When they arrived back at our house, they were out of breath and hungry from their travels," Phyllis explained. "Over a snack, the boys told me about their day's explorations."

Their stories were of a relatively uneventful day, yet Phyllis had trouble believing some of what she heard. She was familiar with the area her sons had been riding through, yet their descriptions did not match what she knew to be there.

"At the corner of Sooke Lake Road and Humpback Road sits Ma Miller's Pub, formerly the Goldstream Inn," said Phyllis. "The Inn's history goes back to the 1860s, but I knew little more than that at the time.

"I had been to the pub for a Sunday brunch, so I knew what the place looked like. While the building the boys described to me was similar to the one I knew, [they claimed] it was larger, and on the wrong side of the road. Also, I knew the road to be paved, not dirt [as the boys reported].

"The boys 'knew' what they had seen, and I 'knew' what I had seen, and we agreed to disagree on what was really there."

The incident may easily have been forgotten, had it not been for Phyllis's volunteer activities at the time. She was working with the Goldstream Region Museum, in the area of collections and displays. One day, out of curiosity, she pulled the archive files on the Goldstream Inn.

Since this photograph of the Goldstream Inn was taken, a fire destroyed all but the main part of the building which, itself, has been drastically altered by time. The wrap-around balcony and corner tower are gone. The original siding hides under thick plaster. Yet, it was this image that three young men saw as they cycled past, one foggy afternoon.

(Photograph courtesy of City of Victoria Archives)

From photographs and a short written history, Phyllis learned that the original Inn had been a large, ornate building, situated opposite its present site. At one point, a fire destroyed a large portion of the Inn, but the main section was saved and moved across the road, where it remained, destined to have its façade drastically altered and its name changed to "Ma Miller's Pub." Phyllis found the photographs of the original Goldstream Inn interesting enough to incorporate them into a display she was working on.

"I had just finished erecting the display when one of the boys paid me a visit at the museum," Phyllis wrote. "He went white when he saw the 1920s photograph of the old Goldstream Inn." The reason for the young man's shocked reaction was that the building in the picture, fronted by rough, unpaved road, was exactly the place he had seen on that foggy October afternoon.

Phyllis's other sons came to view the old photograph, and both identified the building instantly. When Phyllis accompanied all three out to the crossroads for a second look, the boys agreed that the scenery had changed dramatically since the day they had cycled past. It was an eerie situation, and one the three brothers could not explain.

Now, nearly a decade later, Phyllis Griffiths dares to share a theory:

"Encircled by fog, the mysterious mists of time, the boys had travelled back in time some sixty years to pass out again into the place they had come from ... They still recall, with awe, their trip to the ghost of the Goldstream Inn. They all now believe in the reality of time warps and twilight zones."

And so, perhaps, should we.

*****

The stories "The Mists of Time" and "A Time-Shift on Shelbourne Street" are both classic cases of a rare phenomenon known as retrocognition, or postcognition — literally, "backward knowing." People who experience this type of haunting report that their surroundings abruptly change to a scene from the past.

As opposed to someone who sees a ghost who appears displaced in the present time, witnesses of retrocognition seem to be the ones transported back through the years — and sometimes even centuries.

Likely the most famous of all retrocognitive experiences was documented by two English academics, Anne Moberly and Eleanor Jourdain, in their 1911 book, An Adventure. *In it, they wrote of their strange vacation, ten years earlier, in Versailles. During a walk to the Petit Trianon, whose last royal occupant was the doomed queen, Marie Antoinette, both women saw characters and settings which were later determined to have existed in the final days leading up to the French Revolution.*

In the January 1967 edition of the Journal of the American Society for Psychical Research, *psychologist Gardner Murphy theorized that most ghosts are cases of retrocognition, in which the witness has temporarily travelled back in time and been privy to a scene from the past.*

It is interesting food for thought. Is the ghost displaced in your time, or are you in his? Most people who see an apparition aren't likely to consider the experience that objectively for a long time, if ever.

CHAPTER FIVE

The Spooky Standards

British Columbia has been called "Canada's most haunted province." Could it be true? There's no sure way of knowing, but one indicator might be the great number of ghost stories that are both widely known and accepted throughout the province.

Because of their sheer popularity, the following ten tales have been written about previously. Still, no collection of British Columbia ghost stories would be complete without acknowledging the "classics."

Doris Gravlin:
The April Ghost

September 22, 1936, was a pleasant Tuesday evening in Oak Bay, and Doris Gravlin announced that she was going for a walk. In fact, the thirty-year-old private nurse had more on her mind than enjoying some fresh air; she was planning to meet her estranged husband, Victor, at the Oak Bay Beach Hotel. The evening's agenda was to discuss the possibility of a reconciliation.

Victor's alcoholism had caused the Gravlin's two-year separation. By the fall of 1936, it may also have been contributing to a serious mental depression and decline in his physical health. The thirty-six-year-old newspaper sports writer, wanting to change his ways, arranged the evening meeting with his wife.

After leaving the hotel, the couple may have decided to take a stroll along the nearby Victoria Golf Course. The exact details of that walk will never be known, but at around nine o'clock that night, a resident living close to the golf course claimed to have heard a dreadful scream. Doris and Victor Gravlin were never seen alive again.

Five days later, Doris' beaten body was discovered by a caddy who was searching for a lost ball. She was missing some articles of clothing, including the white kid leather shoes she had been wearing at the time of her disappearance.

The local authorities called the case "one of the most mysterious" they had encountered in years. To assist them in the search for the missing Victor Gravlin, they called on police from three other municipalities, as well as the Provincial Force and a corps of Boy Scouts who were used to search the bushy area adjacent to the golf course. In the end, however, it was a fisherman who spotted Victor, just off-shore, floating face down in a web of kelp near the ninth tee. Doris' missing shoes were tucked into the inside pocket of his jacket.

It had been four weeks since the discovery of Doris Gravlin's body, and police were able to close the case; their assumption being that the reconciliation attempt had failed and Victor killed first Doris, then himself, while in a dark, desperate mental state.

The media was willing to let this case slip quietly by — perhaps because Victor had been a popular sports writer for the local newspaper, or perhaps because his uncle still held an executive position there. Doris, however, seemed unwilling to be forgotten. By the following spring, she had returned to the golf course — as a ghost.

If media attention was her goal, her method proved effective. As a phantom, Doris garnered far more publicity than she ever did as a murder victim. In fact, she is often described as "BC's most famous ghost." She certainly is one of its most enduring ones, having appeared countless times in the sixty years since her brutal slaying.

For some unknown reason, she chooses to materialize for a few weeks every spring; thereby earning her most popular nickname — "The April Ghost." She is sometimes seen as a misty grey female shape, skimming effortlessly over the rocky landscape by the water. Other times, she appears very real, dressed in an old-fashioned brown suit, walking on the golf course or standing by the side of the road as if waiting to cross.

Most frequently, however, Doris presents herself in a flowing, white wedding gown, and it is then that her appearances have a sense of purpose. Many times, she has terrified people by appearing in this dress, arms outstretched, rushing toward them at alarming speed. She then melts into a pool of bright light, which vanishes.

According to folklore, young couples who see her this way are destined never to marry. Of course, considering the circumstances of her demise, Doris can hardly be criticized for taking a dim view of marriage.

There has never been any indication that The April Ghost is a threatening presence. Still, witnesses are often quite frightened by the eerie nature of her appearances. When she is seen at close range, her swift and unnatural movements can seem menacing. The ghost's manifestation is usually prefaced with a darkening of mood. No matter how calm and warm the night, the spirit often brings on a rising, directionless wind and clammy coldness. And the very fact that she seems as aware of her human spectators as they are of her can inspire a paranoid fear.

In her book *ESP-ecially Ghosts* (1970), author Eileen Sonin relays the story of a once-sceptical cab driver named George Drysdale who was quite undone by his encounter with the spirit. He was walking along the golf course with his sister and some friends when it happened.

"It was a moonlit night and we could see everything quite clearly," he told Sonin. "I was the first to see a girl standing in front of me and her appearance was so sudden and so frightening that I instinctively turned away. But as I turned, there she was in front of me again. Wherever I turned, she appeared instantly and as if by magic."

The rest of Drysdale's group watched in shock as he appeared to be trapped by the shadowy apparition. Then, in the man's own words, "just as suddenly as she had appeared, she vanished."

After having several years to consider the experience, George Drysdale was no less convinced of what he witnessed. "There is no explanation other than that she was a ghost," he told Sonin. "A human being cannot appear in different places in the twinkling of an eye and vanish the same way. I *know* I saw the ghost of the murdered girl."

In the April 9, 1964 edition of the Vancouver *Province*, a teenager named Anthony Gregson reported being chilled by the unnatural sight of The April Ghost running across the rocks on the beach.

"The ghost moved with much more ease than a human," Gregson told the *Province*. In fact, he described the spectre as a luminous grey shape, gliding swiftly over the landscape, not really touching the ground at all.

Although Anthony Gregson saw the ghost from a much more comfortable distance than did George Drysdale, his reaction was just as strong. "I am not going back there again," he asserted. "It was an unnerving experience."

Even when the ghost appears to be human, she effectively manages to upset any who see her. Often, in the late afternoon, she is seen walking along the golf course, looking unremarkable. People initially take no notice, until they pass her and are filled with an unexplainable sense of dread. As they look over their shoulders, they observe that the strange, lone woman is dressed in a very old-fashioned brown suit — perhaps the outfit Doris Gravlin was wearing in her final hours.

On one occasion, an American tourist and his companion were driving along by the golf course when they believe they saw the ghost in her more human form. They stopped at an intersection and waited while a young woman in a long white dress crossed in front of them, walking toward the sea. Moments later, they stopped at a second intersection, allowing another woman in a flowing white gown to cross in the same direction. Although both the tourist and his friend felt distinctly uncomfortable, neither said a thing.

However, three blocks down the road, when another woman in an identical dress stood watching them approach and waiting to cross the road, the friend was frightened enough to blurt out, "For God's sake, don't stop!" They sped on, rattled and unsure of what they had seen. The next day, listening to a radio talk show, they heard the story of The April Ghost, and were convinced it was Doris they saw repeatedly crossing the road the night before.

Jean Kozocari, an author and self-described "ghost-buster," had been a guest on the talk show that the two men heard. Over the years she had collected so many accounts of this particular spirit, she felt it was time to see it for herself. One spring evening in 1972, Kozocari organized a group of friends to take a walk out on the golf course.

It was a mild evening with no breeze or cloud cover. However, once on the course, the wind picked up suddenly. One member of the group, who was quite accustomed to Kozocari's séances and ghost-hunting expeditions, became markedly upset. As time passed, the wind grew even wilder, and the group decided to go home. As they walked toward the car, someone took Jean Kozocari's hand. She described the experience in the book she co-authored with Robin Skelton, *A Gathering of Ghosts* (1989).

"I remember thinking, 'Poor thing, she really must be frightened; her hand is so cold.' Then, looking ahead, I realized that the whole group was walking ahead of me, and the hand seemed to fade away."

It sounds suspiciously like an encounter with poor, attention-starved Doris Gravlin. The loss of her life was essentially ignored, but the perpetuity of her death can never be forgotten. Her spirited activities keep her in the spotlight as BC's most famous apparition: The April Ghost.

The Good Ghost Photo

On March 5, 1955, a London, England, publication called *Two Worlds* ran a story with the sensational headline "PICTURE OF MAN WHO WASN'T THERE! Colleagues Thought Him Dead — But He Poses with Them!"

The *Two Worlds* article went on to describe and show "an astounding picture," which they deemed "a perfect example of psychic photography." The photograph in question was of the First Legislative Council at New Westminster, British Columbia, and it now hangs in the Parliament Buildings in Victoria. It was taken in either December 1864 or January 1865 — depending upon what you read — and whether it truly is a rare example of a "ghost photograph" has been hotly debated ever since.

The generally accepted story is that the photograph was to include all eleven members of the Council, plus the clerk, Charles Good. It is said, however, that poor health prevented Good from

Look carefully when you count the number of subjects in this 1865 photograph. The eleven members of the First Legislative Council at New Westminster are clearly visible. A twelfth man — the Clerk, Charles Good — is the ghostly image seen second from the right.
(Photograph courtesy of BC Provincial Archives and Records Service)

attending the photograph session. He was so ill, in fact, that rumours of his death had begun to circulate. The rumours proved to be gross exaggerations when Good later recovered and returned to work, but he must have wondered how close to expiring he had really come, when he viewed the photograph taken in his absence.

Standing second from the right on the wooden stairs, between two of the councillors, is the semi-transparent, ghost-like apparition of the supposedly absent clerk. Not only did this appear to be a case of spirit photography, but a most unusual case, as this spirit was still connected to its earthly body at the time.

Over the years, many explanations have been offered. Sources in the *Two Worlds* article suggested that Charles Good, himself, interpreted the strange photograph as a sign that he should change his ways. Although he was the son of a British Reverend, Good was said to be "impetuous and dogmatic in his beliefs." After viewing his own "ghost," however, he supposedly became "serious and thoughtful, markedly tolerant and very devout."

There are others who view the phenomenon as a true case of astral travel. Good's illness may have provided him with a stronger connection to his psychic self. Given that, and the man's strong desire to be present for the photograph, Charles Good may have been able to spiritually project himself into the scene.

Unfortunately, for those who delight in such mysteries, there is a practical explanation which seems to be most likely. The journals of the Legislative Council state that the photograph was taken in January (not December, as is often suggested) and, furthermore, that Charles Good was present and accounted for during all of that month. The reason, then, for the ghostly image can likely be attributed to the photographic techniques of the day. Long time exposures were needed to take a picture, and if Good slipped into the pose a little later than the other eleven men, his image would simply appear to be underexposed.

A divine sign? Astral projection? Or simply a trick of old-fashioned photography? It's no longer possible to inquire at the source. Charles Good eventually retired and returned to England, where he died in 1910 — forty-five years after his "ghost" was captured in the now-famous photograph.

The Presence in Carr House

From mid-May through mid-October, tourists in Victoria are invited to visit 207 Government Street, and tour the birthplace of BC's legendary artist and author, Emily Carr.

One of many landmark sites within walking distance of the Parliament Buildings, Carr House has been painstakingly restored and furnished to accurately represent the period when Emily lived there. And, although it is rare in such historic houses, visitors are invited to sit on the furniture and make themselves feel at home. Ironically, many guests feel strangely uncomfortable doing this.

Emily Carr's mother is said to haunt this house — the birthplace of her famous daughter. If Emily's own spirit roams, it would seem likely one would find it in the Canadian wilds she so vividly recreated on her canvas.

(Photograph courtesy of Barbara Smith)

Alberta author Barbara Smith is an avid student of social history, so she was excited to be seeing Carr House in September of 1995. After having looked forward to the outing for so long, she was surprised that, halfway through the visit, she felt a strong urge to leave.

"As soon as I got to the top of the stairs, I felt *very* uncomfortable," Barbara said. Although her urge was to retreat to the main floor, she was determined to give the upstairs rooms at least a cursory glance.

"The bathroom at the top of the staircase had been restored and looked interesting, but it also looked as though it was someone's everyday bathroom. At the time, I thought that's what made me uncomfortable enough to avoid it.

"Emily's parents' rooms were also re-done, and open. I stuck my head into her mother's room and was greeted with an overwhelming sense that I was intruding in someone's private area. The feeling was so strong that I went back downstairs without even so much as looking in her father's room."

Carr House does have occupants, and there are rooms kept private for their use. Barbara simply assumed she had been too close to these areas, and attributed her discomfort to this. However, she changed her mind soon after talking to the guide.

"The young woman told me that Carr House is haunted — but not by Emily, by her mother," Barbara explained. "She said that few people feel comfortable for long in the mother's bedroom, and that many sense a very strong presence at the top of the stairs. The story is that Emily was afraid to climb the stairs at night, and so her mother would wait for her at the top, holding a candle to light the frightened girl's way."

It would seem that Mrs. Carr remains in this house, where she lived so many years. However, hers is not a "ghostly" presence, according to Barbara Smith.

"I didn't feel those two spots upstairs were haunted, as much as *occupied*," she explained. "It felt more like I'd intruded on a very real person ... or a life currently being lived."

Although she died in 1886, Mrs. Carr obviously remains the "lady of the house," at 207 Government Street.

Ghosts in "Them Thar Hills"

In 1958, a famous BC gold rush town — named for the miner Billy Barker — became a historic park filled with original buildings and antiques from its colourful heyday. Now, nearly forty years later, "Barkerville" is one of the province's leading tourist attractions — and perhaps one of its most haunted places.

Madame Fannie Bendixon's Saloon is one of the many historic buildings on the site. People in the street often assume that an actress has been employed to play the role of Madame Fannie, as they can see a woman in old-fashioned clothing standing in one of the second-storey windows. However, there is no actress — and, more interestingly, no way to possibly access the second floor of the building ... since the staircase collapsed some years ago. Obviously, whoever roams the second floor of the Saloon is not concerned with such earthly limitations.

Barkerville's Theatre Royal is another of the town's ghostly hot spots. Park staff tell stories of mysterious, disembodied footsteps crossing the wooden planks of the stage, and of a woman's humming heard over the public address speakers when the sound system was turned completely off.

The old theatre is even home to an apparition or two. There are reports of an extra person being spotted in the chorus line of one of the productions, several years back. And many actors who have performed on the Theatre Royal stage have shared an odd experience: they will look stage left, in the middle of a show, and notice a strange man standing in the wings. The visitor stands out in his top hat and tails — but when the surprised actor does a double-take, the dashing man disappears in the wink of an eye.

It could be that Barkerville's Theatre Royal, with its subdued lighting and hushed ambiance, provides the perfect atmosphere for spiritual guests. It might be that several of the town's departed residents are fulfilling once-secret dreams of appearing on stage. Or, perhaps there is a less romantic explanation. Apparently, for a period of time after the gold rush, the struggling community that had no real use for a theatre put the building to work as the town morgue.

It is interesting to note that Barkerville's most famous supernatural tale is one of a ghost seen back in 1866, when the town was still booming.

Wellington Delaney Moses was a black man who ran a successful barbershop in Barkerville, every spring through fall. Winters, he spent in the milder climate of New Westminster, and that is where he befriended a well-to-do young American man by the name of Morgan Blessing. In the spring of 1866, Moses and Blessing decided to travel north to the Cariboo gold fields together. En route, they encountered a third man — a down-on-his-luck gambler from Texas called James Barry. It wasn't long before Barry managed to drive a wedge between Moses and Blessing, and the barber was forced to leave the trio and travel on to Barkerville alone.

Later that spring, Wellington Moses took note that while James Barry arrived in Barkerville, his former friend, Morgan Blessing, did not. What was more, Barry's financial fortunes seemed to have improved dramatically. When Barry was asked directly what had become of Morgan Blessing, the gambler denied knowing anything ... but Wellington Moses would soon suspect otherwise.

It was a hot afternoon in June of 1866 when Morgan Blessing walked through the door of his old friend's barbershop. Moses was shocked, but no doubt delighted, to see the man alive. Blessing wasn't looking well, though — his clothes were wet and mouldy, his face, pale and haggard. He had a matted growth of beard on his face and, as he sat in Moses' heavy wooden barber chair, he silently indicated that he wished it shaved off. The barber began by wrapping a hot towel around the man's face and set about stropping his razor. He no sooner started, however, when he saw the towel on his customer's face soak through with blood. The man then vanished into thin air, leaving Moses with a clear message. Morgan Blessing was dead; murdered, most likely, and Wellington Moses believed he knew who the murderer might be. He shared his suspicions with the local law enforcement, but without any evidence of Blessing's death, there was little they could do. Fortunately, they would soon have their proof.

On September 22, 1866, a shallow grave was found at Beaver Pass. In it were Morgan Blessing's badly decomposed remains, showing a single bullet hole in the back of the skull. It didn't take long for the police to arrest James Barry and charge him with the murder. Apparently, the Texas gambler had been foolish enough to give a local girl a large gold nugget scarf pin in the shape of an angel — a pin that was widely known to belong to the late Morgan Blessing.

In July of the following year, Barry was tried, found guilty, and hanged for his crime. Motivated by greed, he had committed murder — and that in itself may not have been uncommon in the wild days of the Cariboo gold rush. What made the case memorable and significant in Barkerville's history was the way the investigation began; with the murdered man himself asking for a shave.

Ratz' Return

In 1893, a young British architect named Francis Mawson Rattenbury became the toast of British Columbia. The cause of his sudden celebrity was his winning design of the province's grand new Parliament Buildings in Victoria.

"Ratz," as he was known, went on in his career to create the Empress Hotel, BC's Government House, Victoria's Crystal Garden, and numerous other landmark buildings. He was the province's most prominent architect, an entrepreneur, and a politician, and the only event that may have upstaged his life was his death.

In 1930, Rattenbury moved back to England with his second wife, Alma. Five years later, the famous architect was murdered; bludgeoned to death by his wife's lover and chauffeur. What followed was one of the most famous trials of the early twentieth century — and the speculation that Rattenbury never quite crossed over to "the other side."

Francis Mawson Rattenbury, once BC's most celebrated architect, was murdered by his wife's young lover, a chauffeur named George Stoner, in 1935.
(Photograph courtesy of BC Provincial Archives and Records Service)

Since the lurid crime that ended his life, there have been rumours that Rattenbury's spirit walks the earth. It has not, however, been spotted in the house at Bournemouth where he died; nor at the Wimbourne Road Cemetery where he is buried. According to those who have met his ghostly presence, Francis Mawson Rattenbury decided, post-mortem, to return to the happier locations of his youth. He is said to haunt the halls of his most celebrated achievement, British Columbia's Parliament Buildings.

Although his death was shrouded in scandal, his life was marked with accomplishment. Understandably, in his afterlife, that is what "Ratz" chooses to remember.

The Haunting of Heron Street

In 1813, a twenty-five-year-old man named John Tod left his native Scotland for the wilds of Canada. He brought with him only three things: a Bible, a book of Robert Burns' poems, and a medical encyclopedia. He sought only *one* thing: adventure with the Hudson's Bay Company. He found it, and became one of the company's most famous traders; known for his bravery when dealing with the native people, if not for his diplomacy when dealing with his own employers.

In 1851, Tod retired to Victoria, where he undertook the construction of a new home on 460 acres of land by the ocean. Interestingly, after thirty-eight dramatic years as a fur trader, a career in politics, seven marriages, and ten children, this rambling house on Heron Street became the most famous and fascinating element of Tod's life — not for its design or its historical significance (although it is considered to be the oldest remaining private home west of the Great Lakes), but for its ghost.

John Tod died in that house in 1882 at the age of ninety-four. His family inherited the 2,000-square-foot dwelling, and eventually sold it. It was then that the ghost became known, for at least two subsequent owners who moved into the house came to believe that it was already somewhat "occupied."

In the kitchen, with its huge stone fireplace, cups and saucers would rattle and move about on their own. Ceramic biscuit jars that were hung on hooks in the stone wall were known to swing wildly to and fro; once for thirty-five continuous minutes, as witnessed by a group of party guests. The cellar door refused to stay shut, no matter how secure the heavy iron latch. Hats were flung from the coat rack, and an antique rocking chair, though usually empty, was rarely still.

In 1944, Colonel Evans and his wife purchased Tod House and moved in. On Christmas day of that year, they awoke to find all their holiday decorations stripped from the walls and the tree, and piled neatly in the centre of the living room floor. The following year, two guests of the Evans' left the house before dawn, after seeing an apparition in their bedroom. They had been sleeping in what Colonel and Mrs. Evans dubbed "the eerie room," one they never felt comfortable enough to spend the night in themselves. In that same bedroom, a window, still nailed solidly in its frame, had once been pushed violently out of the wall, crashing to the ground outside. It was as if something in the room was attempting escape.

With such an abundance of paranormal phenomena, the house was likely destined to achieve fame. Not surprisingly, that's exactly what happened. By the late forties, newspaper accounts and a CBC broadcast ensured that Tod House was nationally known. At one point, a letter addressed simply to "Colonel Evans, The Haunted House, Victoria" found its destination easily.

With fame came speculation, too, about who the ghost of Tod House might be. The first, and least imaginative, guess was that the ghost was John Tod himself. Apparently Tod — who had once carried a Bible across the ocean, to his new homeland — had become quite an atheist in his later years. His request had therefore been a non-Christian burial. His seventh wife, however, was devout and, hoping to save her late husband's soul, had him interred with full ceremony. The common theory was that the haunting was caused by Tod's ensuing displeasure. It was a theory that lost all support, however, by the summer of 1952.

Nineteen fifty-two was the year that Colonel Evans decided to undertake some renovations, including the conversion of the house to oil heat. Two workmen were hired to dig a deep hole for the underground tank but, before they had finished their task, they'd made a gruesome discovery: a human skeleton buried seven feet deep, in the garden. The government anatomist who examined the remains believed them to be those of a native woman. They were so badly decomposed, it was deduced she was buried in quicklime.

Famous Hudson's Bay Company trader and politician John Tod may have taken quite a secret to his grave when he died in 1882 ... for exactly seventy years later, a set of human remains was discovered in the garden of his old home.

The pieces of the ghostly puzzle were beginning to come together. In all likelihood, it was not John Tod who haunted the house, but one of his seven wives; a native woman who was rumoured to have gone insane, causing Tod to confine her to the house. Her bedroom had been the one Colonel and Mrs. Evans called "the eerie room;" the same one in which the window had exploded outward; the same one in which the two overnight guests had seen an apparition. Apparently, that apparition had been the image of a dark-haired woman, bound in chains and iron shackles, her arms outstretched and her lips moving in a soundless plea for help.

Following the discovery of the unmarked grave, Tod House faded from the public eye. It is difficult to find any mention of it, even in local newspapers, until June of 1974, when the Oak Bay Municipal Council declared it to be a heritage landmark. The designation meant that no unapproved changes could be made to the house — but the greatest change had already taken place, more than twenty years earlier. That was in 1952, when the woman's remains were taken from the grounds of Tod House and granted a decent burial. All paranormal activity came to an abrupt stop that day.

It was the end of the haunting on Heron Street.

The Headless Brakeman

The fictional locale of Sleepy Hollow has nothing on Vancouver, when it comes to producing legends of headless spectres. In 1928, at the CPR yards on Granville Street, an unfortunate railway brakeman named Hub Clark failed to keep his head, but managed to secure his place in local folklore.

It was (of course) a dark and stormy night when Hub slipped and fell on the tracks, knocking himself unconscious. Moments later, a passenger train came along, and the man was decapitated.

Since then, tales abound of a headless man in overalls being seen around the rail yard on rainy nights. Perhaps Hub is looking for his head — or hoping to warn others who might slip in the treacherous mud near the tracks.

The Ghostly Gallery

In the days when every grand home had its own proper name, the Burnaby Art Gallery was known as "Fairacres, The Ceperley Mansion."

The glorious thirty-six-room Edwardian structure was built as a retirement home by Henry Ceperley and his wife, Grace. Over the great oak fireplace, they had carved the inscription *"The ornament of a house is the friends who frequent it,"* and Henry Ceperley certainly did enjoy spending his real estate and insurance fortune entertaining friends from the city.

The lavish parties were not really Grace's style, however. She was a quiet woman who seemed happiest feeding the wild birds and tending the garden. Another of her simple pleasures in life was doting on children, a fact that was evident when her will was probated after her death in 1919. She left Fairacres (which was in her name) to her husband, but with one provision: when Henry either died or sold the place, she wished the proceeds to be used to build a children's playground in Stanley Park.

Henry Ceperley did sell the home, in 1922, but for reasons unknown, the terms of Grace's will were never met. In what was to become the long, sad history of the property, this was but the first offense.

In the forty-five years that followed, Fairacres was destined to house a parade of tenants — and not all would treat her kindly or bring positive energy to the house. There were two private owners following the Ceperleys, then a stint as a tuberculosis ward for Vancouver General Hospital. When that suffering moved elsewhere, the home went briefly to another private buyer. Then, in 1939, began a fifteen-year tenure as a monastery for an order of Benedictine monks. In 1954, the monks moved to a new abbey, and Fairacres moved on to what were inarguably its darkest days.

He called himself "Archbishop John I," and his church, the "Temple of the More Abundant Life." But according to the warrants issued for his arrest on charges of bigamy, assault, and extortion, the man's real name was William Franklin Wolsey, his many diplomas were fakes, and his religion no more than a cultish excuse for the abuse of its members — many of whom were small children.

For several years, Archbishop John conducted his atrocities in the spacious rooms of Fairacres. Children of the Temple's school were taught that they would die if they did not believe what was taught them in the classroom. Youngsters who displeased or disappointed the archbishop in any way were subject to the cruellest of punishments, and *every* child was forced to participate in the unorthodox "Sex and Hygiene" course, which Archbishop John taught personally.

By the time Wolsey was exposed and the church collapsed, inestimable damage had been done to the cult members, their innocent children, and perhaps to Fairacres, as well. But the great home had not seen the last of its trauma.

It was the mid-sixties — a time of riot and rebellion — when the house was used by Simon Fraser University as a dormitory. In a time when tradition was shunned for the alternative of "doing your own thing," the glorious architecture and craftsmanship of the house could not have been less respected or appreciated. But mere disrespect turned to outright vandalism when the students were threatened with eviction in 1966. Barricades were erected, psychedelic graffiti spray-painted throughout, and a bonfire was lit on the hardwood floor of the billiard room.

Eventually, the siege ended, and the damage was repaired. But by 1967, when the house opened to the public as the Burnaby Art Gallery, it was becoming obvious that what could not be restored was Fairacre's injured spirit. It had become an unhappy house; a haunted one.

The reports began with a night watchman who was checking the third floor on his regular rounds. What he saw was a woman, thought to be Grace Ceperley, floating down the hallway in a long, flowing, white, transparent gown. Since then, she has been witnessed on many occasions, often in white, sometimes in a wispy grey or blue evening dress. Occasionally, Grace prefers being heard to being seen, and will manifest as the rustling sound of satin or crinoline, accompanied by an overwhelming chill and the eerie intuition that someone is trying to communicate. On December 15, 1985, *Province* reporter Damian Inwood wrote about the gallery and quoted one woman who had had such an experience. "I knew it was something supernatural," she said. "I didn't feel I could deal with it."

There were many who didn't feel they could deal with it. In the October 31, 1986 edition of the *Vancouver Sun*, the Burnaby Art Gallery's director, Roger Boulet, admitted as much. "People are uncomfortable in the building," he said. "No one likes to stay late by themselves." Boulet himself resigned two months later, and devoted fully one-third of his final year-end report to the hauntings. "While this situation may be taken lightly by the Board," he wrote, "it *is* a matter of concern when staff are not willing to work in the evening."

It is little wonder, especially since Grace's apparition was not the only evidence of Fairacre's otherworldly populace.

A woman named Maria Guerrero worked in an office on the second floor. For some time, she thought nothing of the constant creaking footsteps above her head, or of the loud, distinct sounds of furniture being moved and windows opened and closed. She simply assumed someone lived upstairs — but then, one day, learned the truth; that the third floor had been abandoned years before. It was empty, but for its ghostly inhabitants.

Equally haunted was Fairacre's basement, a dark, eerie place where tools that were in use would be replaced on the wall rack the very moment the handyman's back was turned, and heavy padlocks swung to and fro on the storage room door. In 1987, CBC cameras toured the building with psychic Joan Fontaine. The woman appeared particularly uncomfortable in the basement, where she claimed to sense children crying for help. "This is a very unhappy place," Fontaine said, in the October 31,

1987 edition of the *Vancouver Sun*. Much of the darkness seemed to be connected to the Temple of the More Abundant Life.

It raises an interesting question. Could the unhappiness of the abused youngsters have drawn back the spirit of Grace Ceperley, a woman who loved children? Perhaps. Or perhaps, unaware of their desperation, Grace simply walks the halls of her beloved home to protest the disregard of her last will and testament. It's a mystery that will never be solved in Burnaby's "gallery of ghosts."

A Lady in Blue

When Point Ellice House was built in the late 1860s by Peter and Caroline O'Reilly, it must have been one of the finest dwellings in Victoria. Today, its fifteen rooms serve as a museum, and perhaps as home to one of the city's gentle spirits.

The O'Reillys raised three children in Point Ellice House, and Kathleen, their only daughter, remained unmarried and lived in her treasured childhood home until her death in 1945. Some say she even stayed beyond.

In 1967, Peter O'Reilly's grandson, John, opened Point Ellice as a private museum. Soon after, visitors began telling John and his wife, Inez, what they had suspected all along; their home was haunted.

One angry woman complained that the ghost had frightened her little grandchild. It is more likely that the girl was simply *startled*, as the spirit of Kathleen O'Reilly always appeared to be benevolent and helpful.

Some visitors have mentioned a woman matching Kathleen's description, dressed in a blue period dress, conducting tours of the house. No such living guide existed at the time. Once, two men reported Kathleen waiting to greet them when they arrived. When they later left, she appeared to follow them down the road.

When the provincial government took over operation of the museum in 1974, Kathleen stopped making appearances. Perhaps with no O'Reillys living on the premises, she no longer feels at home in beautiful Point Ellice House.

Eerie Art: The Hetty Fredrickson Story

It was December of 1965 when Hetty and Douglas Fredrickson moved into a twelve-room home on Williams Street in Chilliwack. Only months later, they would move back out, following one of the strangest and most unsettling experiences of their lives.

In the beginning, they noticed odd things happening during the day. There were sounds of breathing and of footsteps on the stairs, the sudden, overwhelming scent of perfume, and bureau drawers that refused to stay shut in an unused bedroom. One night, Hetty saw the misty, glowing shape of a person in that same bedroom. These incidents were certainly frightening enough, but what began to truly disturb Hetty was the powerfully vivid, recurring nightmare she began to experience.

In the dream, she saw the body of a woman lying on the attic floor. She wore a bright, cotton dress — red with large yellow flowers — and her expression was one of pure terror. Night after night, Hetty suffered this vision. Finally, she decided to deal with it the only way she knew how. She was an artist; she would paint what she saw in her nightmare.

Eventually, she elected to combine the images of the dream-woman and of the ghost she had seen in the upstairs bedroom. Having frustratingly few details of the spirit's appearance, Hetty chose to leave half of the face in her portrait blank. After many days, the painting was complete, and its artist hoped that the creative process had somehow exorcised the supernatural beings from the house.

She hoped in vain.

It was no more than a week later when Hetty Fredrickson examined her own painting and noticed something unbelievable.

The portrait — without having been touched — was beginning to change. The blank portion of the face was filling itself in, showing the discernible features of a man, right down to his moustache.

Few people knew about it, but reports of the haunted painting began to circulate around Chilliwack. Similarly, stories of the house's history began to find their way back to Hetty. An old man who had lived there once committed suicide, she was told. Legend had it a woman was murdered and then bricked up in the chimney. The Fredricksons didn't know if the tales were true, but they did know that their own experiences were real. The footsteps, the breathing sounds, the perfume, and moving furniture all persisted. The painting continued to have a life of its own. A thorough exploration of the house turned up a hidden door, a boarded-over passageway, and a small, previously undiscovered turret room. Hetty and Douglas began to wonder what sort of past was hidden within their own home.

Apparently, others were wondering as well. Publicity about the mysterious, mercurial painting had continued to grow, as did the numbers of curious visitors to the house. One Sunday afternoon in June of 1966, nearly 700 sightseers deluged the Fredricksons. The weight of those standing by the front door alone collapsed the old wooden porch. For weeks, it was estimated that an average of 200 cars cruised down Williams Street, past "the ghost house" every day.

Ultimately, it was not the ghosts that drove the Fredricksons away; it was the tourists. Hetty and Douglas packed their things and moved to Sayward, a small town on Vancouver Island. They took the strange painting, but left the haunting behind them.

The publicity eventually died down, but paranormal activity at the Fredrickson's old house continued through the years. Subsequent tenants claimed to encounter several ghosts, including one malevolent presence that would frighteningly immobilize people for several minutes. A delivery person was once so terrified by the sudden, supernatural appearance of a woman and a baby on the porch of the house, she simply dropped her packages and ran.

However many spirits inhabited the house on Williams Street, they are all homeless now. The building burned to the ground several years ago, leaving nothing but ashes and the memory of one of BC's most famous hauntings.

CHAPTER SIX

The Dunsmuir Homes

Every year, hundreds of thousands of tourists pass through them, eager to experience a taste of the opulent past.

Their impressive exteriors and lavish interiors have made them favourite location choices for the film and television industry.

They are two of Victoria's most significant landmarks: Craigdarroch Castle and Hatley Park; the architectural legacy of a family called Dunsmuir.

Robert Dunsmuir was a fiery Scottish immigrant who made his fortune in Vancouver Island coal. His eldest son, James, rose to prominence as the province's premier, and later, lieutenant-governor. Their wives became famous in their own rights for successfully entertaining the cream of Victorian society; their daughters, for making ambitious marriages.

The Dunsmuirs were a colourful, power-hungry, flawed, and often-feuding family who contributed considerably to the history books with their business dealings and personal dramas, and to the Victoria skyline with their ostentatious homes.

A century later, the vibrant Dunsmuir spirit lives on in those homes — according to some stories, quite literally.

Craigdarroch: Castle for a Coal Baron

To his detractors, he was known as "King Grab"; a greedy capitalist who made his fortune by keeping politicians in his pocket and impoverished workers under his thumb. But even his worst critic was bound to acknowledge one fact: Robert Dunsmuir, British Columbia's infamous millionaire coal baron, built his impressive empire from scratch.

In 1851, Dunsmuir and his young family were newcomers to Vancouver Island and their home reflected their status as poor immigrant workers. It was the roughest of log cabins — cramped, cold, lacking even the small luxury of a window. Years later, when Dunsmuir's status changed to that of the province's richest man, he would once again have a home that reflected his lot. He made certain of it.

What Robert Dunsmuir built was a castle, the ultimate monument to his power and wealth. It would have four floors plus a tower, thirty-nine rooms, and eighteen fireplaces. Ceilings would be ornately painted with flowers, birds, bees, and cherubs, windows, magnificently decorated with stained glass. The finest oak, walnut, mahogany, and cedar would be used to panel the interior, and the best granite, marble, and sandstone made up the exterior walls. Eighty-seven steps up the impressive main staircase would lead to a fourth-floor dance hall that was easily large enough to contain a three-bedroom house. It would be impressive.

The creation of "Craigdarroch," as he would name it, should have been Dunsmuir's moment in the sun, but instead, the castle was built in the shadow of tragedy.

Construction of Craigdarroch Castle began in Victoria in late 1887. Fewer than four months later the architect, Warren

Robert and Joan Dunsmuir. A certain grim determination in their faces may explain how this immigrant couple rose from a Spartan log cabin to the luxury of Craigdarroch Castle.

(Photographs courtesy of BC Provincial Archives and Records Service)

Heywood Williams, died of an enlargement of the heart. He would never see his forty-fourth birthday or the completion of the most impressive project of his career.

Fifteen months later, in April of 1889, sixty-three-year-old Robert Dunsmuir retreated to his bedroom, suffering from a terrible cold. Within four days, the man believed to be in perfect health was in a coma. Two days after that, "King Grab" was mysteriously dead. Craigdarroch Castle, the symbol of all he had achieved, was still one year away from completion.

There were more funerals to come. In September of 1889, forty-year-old Agnes, the second Dunsmuir daughter, died of the typhoid fever that swept through Nanaimo. In March of the following year, Agnes' husband, James Harvey, passed away, having never regained his health after nursing his wife and children through the epidemic.

In the summer of 1890, Craigdarroch was finally ready for occupancy. There was likely little celebration, however, as Dunsmuir's grieving widow, Joan, her orphaned grandchildren, and three unmarried daughters moved in.

The king of Craigdarroch Castle was gone, but "Queen Joan" determinedly took her place in Victoria's grandest home. Society parties were hosted and lavish weddings were held. For eighteen years, Craigdarroch housed all the Dunsmuir dramas and events.

Then, in October of 1908, Joan Dunsmuir died. The contents of Craigdarroch were auctioned off and the castle, itself, was sold, ending an era in British Columbia's history.

After Joan's death, the castle's own existence would be frequently threatened in the decades to come. It was too large and expensive for most people to take on as a private residence, yet inappropriately designed for institutional use. Yet, an institution is what it was destined to become.

The castle served first as a veterans' hospital, following World War I. By 1921, the government chose to move the patients of "Craig Darroch Military Hospital" into a larger institution, and the castle was taken over by Victoria College. In 1946, the College had record enrolment and was deemed to be a dangerously over-crowded fire hazard. The students moved out and the school board, wondering what to do with its condemned investment, moved in. For the next twenty years, Robert Dunsmuir's castle was filled with text books, a maze of little offices, and unflattering fluorescent lights.

By the time the school board left in 1967, seeking roomier accommodations, Craigdarroch had fallen into a severe state of disrepair. Wood was rotting, stone was crumbling, and bits of broken stained glass were left un-repaired. The castle was threatened with demolition — some people feeling a high-rise apartment would be an improvement to the site — but one last tenant was to provide a stay of execution. The Victoria School of Music took up residence for the next decade, then delivered the building safely into the hands of The Castle Society — a group determined to see Craigdarroch restored and respected as an important historic landmark and museum.

At this point, the physical changes to the building were significant; hand-decorated ceilings had been painted over, large rooms had been partitioned into many tiny offices, and thousands of people had left as many necessary repairs behind. But even as the restoration began, it became obvious that the psychic imprint left by Craigdarroch's many tenants would not be so easily erased.

One of the workers hired to return the castle to its former glory reported having a most unusual experience, one day, as he rested after lunch. The man had found a comfortable chair facing the stairway, and was enjoying a tranquil break before he had to return to his job. He was contented, and feeling a bit sleepy, when a sudden, strange sight on the stairs captured his attention.

In its days as Victoria College, Craigdarroch saw countless social dances, and its lovely staircase provided the dramatic backdrop for many young women intent on making grand entrances. What the startled worker saw, that afternoon, would seem to be a sort of partial "memory" of one of these events.

It was the vision of a woman's small foot, dressed in a satin shoe. The shoe peeked out from beneath a lovely gown, which trailed behind on each step as, in smooth slow motion, the apparition descended the stairs. This carried on for several minutes, but oddly, the rest of the woman never appeared. Only the one satin shoe, and a length of gown.

It seemed that once Craigdarroch Castle was freed from the clutter of offices and the distraction of students, its ghosts were more easily noticed. As it began to operate as a museum, the past quite literally came to life.

"Psychics have sensed presences, here," one guide admitted, adding that they are presences not everyone seems to be comfortable with. Apparently the odd visitor to Craigdarroch will walk in the castle, then walk straight back out, not sure what has caused their sudden unease. The castle's staff might be able to explain; many have had supernatural experiences of their own.

Some encountered sudden, cold gusts of air — perhaps not remarkable in such an old building, except that they would happen even on the warmest of summer days. There were the occasional ghostly strains of piano music, and the strong smell of candle-wax, first thing in the morning, although no candles were ever burned.

One guide "officially" denied that the castle was haunted, then went on to describe the apparition of a little girl who had been seen in the basement, and the sensation of two suffering soldiers in one of the bedrooms. "Most people find that a painful room," he explained. "I know I do." It would seem that although Craigdarroch only spent two short years as a veterans' hospital, it did not survive the experience unscathed.

Most of the castle's spirits seem happy enough, however. They appear involved in the activities of their own time, and quite unaware of the modern world. One woman, employed at Craigdarroch for quite some time, reported several experiences with these "people from the past."

On one occasion, she attended a lecture that was held at the castle. A coffee break was taken in the middle of the event, and the room emptied as people took the opportunity to stretch their legs and explore the building. When nearly everyone had left, the woman saw a maid dressed in a Victorian-style uniform enter the room and hastily look both ways. She then vanished, before the woman's eyes.

Another time, the woman was present as the castle was being closed for the night. A friend, described as being "slightly psychic," expressed concern that the doors were being locked while one visitor was still inside. "What about that man in the bowler hat?" she asked, pointing to what everyone else agreed was a very empty chair.

It is not at all surprising that one of the strongest presences at Craigdarroch Castle is considered to be the original lady of the house: Joan Dunsmuir. Although she has never been seen, her spirit seems to occupy the second floor suite of rooms where she spent most of her final years. Indeed, she seems to be stubbornly protective of that space.

"Once there was a display case set up in Joan's sitting room," one long-time castle employee recalled. "It had a top hat and a walking-stick or umbrella or something in it. I remember that the display was fine when the castle was locked up for the night, but the next morning, both the hat and stick had been knocked off the stand *inside the glass case!*"

Those present agreed that Joan was indicating that the sitting-room was her realm, and that others should keep their things out of it.

There is a legend that says Robert Dunsmuir built Craigdarroch Castle to fulfill a promise to the strong-willed woman who was his wife. It seems much more likely that he built it as a symbol of his own success. Still, the castle was very important to Joan. She was an original pioneer; a woman who started out sweeping a dirt floor in a crude log cabin. It is little wonder that once she got her castle, she was reluctant to leave it, even in death.

There are many spirits who seem to have made it their eternal home, but Joan Dunsmuir remains the queen of Craigdarroch Castle.

Hatley Park:
The Next Generation

In the days before sensational tabloid newspapers lined every supermarket check-out, the failings and feuds of the Dunsmuir family managed to keep the public happily entertained.

Their youngest son, Alex, was a hopeless alcoholic who scandalously lived for nearly twenty years with an American divorcee. Daughter Anne Euphemia spent more than half of her life in insane asylums, and would finally die in one. Granddaughter Dola became a nearly constant party companion to the outrageous Hollywood actress, Tallulah Bankhead. Dola's older sister, Kathleen, squandered her fortune trying to invent a Hollywood career of her own. The Dunsmuirs had famous friends, questionable business ethics, too much money and considerably less taste — and people loved to hear about them.

One can imagine, then, the absolute sensation caused by a headline in the *New York Times*, no less, on November 10, 1901.

PREMIER OF BRITISH COLUMBIA SUED BY HIS MOTHER

The province's premier at that time was James Dunsmuir. His mother, Joan, had taken him to court to contest the will of her younger son, Alex.

Alex had died at the young age of forty-six — officially, of meningitis, but more likely of alcoholic poisoning — and left his portion of the Dunsmuir fortune to his older brother, James. Joan felt that her son's wealth should have reverted to her. The Dunsmuir daughters, who relied upon generous financial gifts from their mother, agreed. The result was a five-year legal battle that would divide the family and exhaust every appeal all the way to London's Privy Council. In the end, the will was upheld. James

James and Laura Dunsmuir. He fancied himself a gentleman farmer; she loved to play "society hostess." Hatley Park, their magnificent country mansion, served both ambitions.
(Photographs courtesy of BC Provincial Archives and Records Service)

won his case, but lost in every effort he made to reconcile with his family.

When the court case ended, James pursued plans to build himself a retirement home. Given the timing and his probable state of mind, it is not surprising that he wanted a design that was larger, grander, and more impressive than Craigdarroch Castle. He hired architect Samuel Maclure and instructed him to spare no expense. Maclure was simply to build what James Dunsmuir wanted.

Apparently, James wanted a great deal, for "Hatley Park," as he would call it, would out-do every private residence ever built in the province. It was a massive medieval castle with Tudor additions, built to appear as if it had existed for centuries. There were twenty-two bedrooms and nine baths, and a magnificent top-floor ballroom. A staff of twelve tended to the house, alone, and a veritable village of workers were employed to care for the gardens, greenhouses, and livestock. It was spectacular; James Dunsmuir's own castle. And, unlike his father, James lived long enough to enjoy it. He and his wife, Laura, moved in in 1908.

Hatley must have meant a great deal to Laura, as well. She was a woman in love with prestige and social position, and the grand scale upon which she could entertain at Hatley Park surely secured her place in Victorian society. After James died in 1920, Laura continued to live in her beloved mansion. She stayed on, in fact, until her own death in 1937 — and perhaps even beyond.

When it went up for sale, Hatley Park, like Craigdarroch Castle before it, became a bit of a white elephant. Laura Dunsmuir, herself, had spent most of the Depression years struggling to maintain the expensive residence. It was far too much for any private buyer, and ill-suited for many institutional purposes. For four years, Hatley sat empty, cared for by a skeleton staff.

During this time, one of the maids began experiencing rather strange sensations. They were strong enough that she felt obliged to report them to her superior, particularly since they had begun to interfere with her work. It seems the woman had the intense feeling that someone was watching her as she went about her chores. At first she shrugged it off, assuming it was the result of working alone in a large, empty building. Her nervousness seemed to increase daily, however, and soon she was so affected by her unease that she was unable to enter certain rooms by herself. It seemed that Hatley Park was haunted.

The possibility of a ghost was likely of little concern to the great home's eventual buyer, however. In 1940, the Department of Defence purchased the estate for a mere $75,000, intending to turn it into a military academy. If anyone was even aware of the strange presence in Hatley Park, it is doubtful that that knowledge would have kept the government from taking advantage of such a real estate bargain.

The deal was made, and in 1941 the Dunsmuir mansion became Royal Roads Military College. Cadets were brought in to train, and almost immediately, the stories began to circulate.

Predictably, students who studied late into the night were the first to encounter the ghost. It was described as being overcome by the eeriest of sensations — as if webs of icy thread were being brushed across one's skin. Interestingly, it always occurred on the upper floors, where the increasingly weak Laura Dunsmuir was confined, late in life.

If there was any doubt that it was Laura who haunted her home of nearly thirty years, it was likely removed when cadets began reporting an apparition. Occasionally, the young men would wake in the middle of the night to see a little old woman standing beside their beds. In one isolated instance, the student was awakened when he felt a tugging on his leg. He was shocked to see a strangely transparent old lady literally trying to yank him from his bed. The young man tried to pull free, but the ghost held fast. The harder he shook his leg, the harder she held on. Finally, with one mighty move, he was able to free himself. As soon as he did, the spirit vanished.

One could assume Laura did not appreciate having her lovely home filled with loud young men.

In 1994, Royal Roads Military College fell victim to federal budget cuts. In September of 1995, it reopened as Royal

Roads University, a civilian school offering degrees in business, technology, and environmental management. How Laura Dunsmuir's spirit feels about the change remains to be seen, but sooner or later, some industrious student burning the midnight oil is sure to encounter her: a vigilant old lady, caring for her beloved home into eternity.

CHAPTER SEVEN

Unfinished Business: Messages from Beyond

In a Hollywood career that spanned more than four decades, actress Ida Lupino likely never had a more dramatic experience than one particular phone call she received from her father. He had called to tell her where she would find the final papers needed to settle his estate; a timely issue, considering the man had been dead for six months.

*****

A doctor, driving through a blinding rainstorm in 1920s rural Saskatchewan, was shocked to see his long-dead wife suddenly appear on the hood of his Model T. He brought the car to a screeching halt — just in time to avoid what would have surely been a fatal collision with a freight train.

*****

When a deceased loved one appears, or communicates in some way from beyond the grave, there often seems to be a motive. While other hauntings may have very little personal meaning to the people who witness them, visits from late family members or close friends can be quite purposeful. It has often been reported that the spirit of someone dear provided a warning or diversion, when disaster was imminent.

On occasion, the ghost appears to fulfill a promise, or provide necessary information. The numerous accounts of people having a psychic "communication" with someone, unaware that they are, at that moment, dying, can lead to the conclusion that the visits are often to simply bid farewell. Also common are reports of loved ones returning in some form to provide comfort or guidance. Interestingly, "comfort" is a word often associated with these incidents.

Other brushes with the paranormal may leave people upset and even frightened, but being visited by someone who was loving in life usually inspires a sense of peace. Many recall their experience as special, and are left reassured that the departed one is in a happy place, and that they, themselves, are being watched over by a caring spirit.

Many British Columbians have had such experiences. Most involve a close friend or relative; all have to do with the delivery of an important message "from beyond."

The first two stories concern spirits who seem intent upon taking care of unfinished business.

The Gift

Dawn Scott was a young woman who must have considered herself very fortunate. Not only did she have a boyfriend with whom she was deeply in love, but the other important man in her life, her father, thought highly of the young man, as well.

Perhaps the usual paternal possessiveness was set aside because Dawn's father had enjoyed a very close relationship with *his* wife's father. In fact, before he died, Dawn's grandfather had given her father a special gift; a pocket knife.

"My father treasured it with all his might," wrote Dawn. "Wherever he went, the knife would be right along there with him."

He was understandably upset, then, when the knife went missing, during the winter of 1988. A thorough search was made, but the beloved knife could not be found.

Not long after, Dawn's father was out of town when he recalled that he may have dropped the knife by the wharf, back in Nelson. He called home and asked if Dawn's boyfriend would mind going down there to take a look.

"My boyfriend and my father liked one another very much," Dawn explained, "and to please my father was something my boyfriend always liked to do." The young man went down to the wharf and searched for an hour but, unfortunately, found nothing. He was upset, feeling that he had let the older man down. Dawn's father, though disappointed, thanked him and told him not to worry.

Two months later, the loss of the pocket knife was likely put into perspective when real tragedy struck. Dawn's boyfriend was killed in a terrible car accident. Her entire family shared her grief, particularly her father, who felt he had lost a good friend.

Early one morning, two weeks after the young man's death, Dawn and her mother were awakened by her father's startled cries.

"I came running out of my room," she recalled. "My father's face was white. He was shaking all over. I could tell he was on the verge of tears." When he calmed down enough to explain what had happened, the story that came out was astonishing.

He told Dawn and her mother that Dawn's boyfriend had come to visit him while he slept. He clearly saw him sit down on the edge of the bed and heard him as he said his goodbyes.

"My mother tried telling him it was just a dream, just nonsense. But my father wouldn't listen," Dawn wrote. And then he told them something even more unbelievable.

"He finally said ... very calmly and serenely ... that my boyfriend had returned his pocket knife."

Dawn's eyes met her mother's. They shook their heads sadly; obviously, Dawn's father was upset, perhaps even delusional. But suddenly, the distraught man turned his closed hand palm-up and opened his fingers. Dawn will never forget what she saw.

"In his hand lay the pocket knife my grandpa had given my father as a gift before he died."

Returning the treasure, and thereby performing one final favour, was a gesture of friendship extended from beyond the grave.

The Debt

Daisy Bligh of Victoria considered her grandson, Trevor, a responsible young man. He took his debts seriously; commendable for anyone, but even more so for Trevor because of his sad circumstances. He was dying.

One day he expressed concern to his mother. "What if I die before [the debt] is paid up?" A religious woman, she assured him that should that happen, the Lord would look after the matter.

Trevor did die, in November of 1994, and his payments were not yet finished. His grieving mother, knowing her son would want the matter taken care of, began to collect his assets.

There was a little spare cash that Trevor had, plus some cheques that were due him. Then it was discovered that an insurance package from his mother's place of employment would be sending a benefit. When the insurance money arrived, a sizable amount of interest had been added to the expected sum.

When all the monies were pooled, Trevor's family was amazed to note that the total came to exactly three dollars more than the debt he owed. They would be more amazed when they bought the money order needed to send to the lender.

It came to exactly three dollars.

Whether through divine assistance or a profound sense of responsibility that extended even beyond Trevor's life, the debt was repaid in full.

*****

Daisy Bligh also sent the following story, which came from a member of her church. It is the first of three accounts in which people are visited by, or experience a vision of, a relative at the moment of death.

Surrounded by Angels

A woman whose father was slowly dying in an extended care hospital had neglected her own life to spend as much time as possible with him. When it came time for a dental appointment which had been made many months earlier, she debated whether she should cancel it, as she had other commitments.

"Go," the nurses urged her. "Get your teeth done. You've been here for him so much — do this one thing for yourself."

The woman decided to keep the appointment. As she sat waiting in the dentist's chair, her eyes closed, she had a startlingly clear vision of the hospital room her father was in. She could see him lying peacefully in his bed — and standing guard at each corner of the bed was an angel.

Shocked by the suddenness and clarity of the image, she phoned the hospital immediately after her appointment.

"Yes," she was sadly informed. Her father had died. His time of death: exactly when the woman envisioned him, surrounded by angels.

Grandmother's Visit

By the fall of 1933, the Great Depression was in full swing. Earning a living had become a challenge, even for young, able-bodied men — which may have been the reason Gordon Sculthorpe was willing to spend a decidedly unpleasant winter managing a trap line.

The line was situated north of Fort St. John, in less than hospitable terrain. In any season, it could only be reached by pack pony. Once the snow arrived, a dogsled was needed to travel up and down the line, collecting the furs.

The accommodations were less than luxurious, as well. Gordon made his home in a tiny log cabin, its walls chinked with mud and moss in a vain effort to keep out the minus-thirty-degree winter temperatures. Food supplies were stored in a cache, high atop a pole, so the animals wouldn't ravage them.

Perhaps the worst of it was the isolation. Gordon Sculthorpe's trap line started fifty miles from the nearest outpost. He had no human contact that entire winter, not even mail delivery that would have comforted him with letters from home and news of the outside world. Gordon would have loved to hear from his brothers and sister, his parents, or his grandmother.

Considering this desire, he may have believed what he experienced, one winter night, to be the invention of his lonely mind. He described the incident to author Sheila Hervey in *Canada Ghost to Ghost* (1996).

"One night in January ... something woke me up. I was really awake, because I got up onto my elbow. And there was my grandmother standing in the doorway! I asked 'What is the matter?' She smiled, and then slowly faded away."

Three months later, spring arrived and warmer temperatures allowed a visit to the outpost. When Gordon arrived, he picked up his mail, which had been collecting for him all that winter.

One letter from home contained sad news. The previous fall, after Gordon left to work on the trap line, his grandmother had unexpectedly taken ill. Within weeks, she passed away.

Gordon was shocked by the news, and even more so by the date of his grandmother's death. It occurred the same night her image appeared before him in the lonely, isolated, trapper's cabin.

Unable to say goodbye in a conventional fashion, the woman had crossed time, space, and even death to see her grandson one last time.

A Promise Kept

In the pioneering days of the 1800s, many Eastern Canadian families were divided when sons and daughters moved west to settle their own piece of land.

Kay Corbett of Victoria recalls that her paternal grandparents did just that — left their homes in Quebec and Ontario to stake a claim near Metchosin, on the southern tip of Vancouver Island. Their son — Kay's father — Lee Llewellyn Field, was born on that farm in 1882, far from the grandmother in Quebec who celebrated his arrival.

According to Kay, the woman "yearned to see the grandson who lived on the other side of the continent, and made a vow that she would get to see him before she died." However, the more years that went by, the more Lee's grandmother's health failed, and the more improbable the long train voyage became.

It was 1897 when word came from Quebec that the elderly woman's life was near its end. Lee was fifteen years old, nearly a man, and it seemed that he would never meet his grandmother.

One night soon after, Lee awoke, sensing that someone had touched him. When he opened his eyes, he saw a kind face he knew only from photographs. It was his grandmother, standing by the bed, looking down upon him. The vision frightened him so, he yanked the bed covers over his head and remained under them until morning.

When Lee sat down to breakfast that morning, the experience of the night before was still very much on his mind. He was trying to explain to the family, when a telegram arrived. It contained sad news; Lee's grandmother had passed away. The Field family was stunned — not by the woman's death; that had been expected — but, rather, by the fact that her death had occurred the night before, at the exact time Lee woke to find her gazing down at him.

"My dad had a strong faith," Kay Corbett wrote, many years later, "and believed that he was always surrounded by good spirits looking after him."

His was a faith that was no doubt strengthened, and perhaps even initiated, by a loving grandmother who believed in keeping her promises.

Bill Drops In

There are many who believe that our loved ones continue to guide and comfort us long after they have passed from this plane of existence. The people who provided the following three tales must certainly agree.

Stan McKinnon has spent his entire working life in the weekly newspaper field, and proudly wears the fifty-year pin from the Canadian Newspapers Association. Due to decades of journalism experience, Stan is, by his own admission, more inclined to be sceptical than credulous. However, a supernatural visit he had in 1955 is something he still cannot explain, and describes as "a very distinct experience."

At that time, Stan was editor of the *Surrey Leader*, and secretary-treasurer of its publishing company. G.W.A. "Bill" Smith was the founder of the paper, and its publisher. He was also a man Stan respected and considered to be a good friend, and many enjoyable hours were spent socializing in the Smiths' large apartment, on the second floor of the Leader building.

"Because of ill health," Stan recalled, "Bill Smith was not able to work on the paper for the last two years of his life." Still, he maintained a great interest in the paper he had created.

The paper went to press on Wednesdays, and every Tuesday evening, Stan McKinnon would be working late, doing the final paste-up on the pages. But he never spent those evenings alone.

"Even when he was very ill, Bill Smith would come down about 9:00 p.m. ... pour us both a rye, and see how things were progressing on the weekly issue." It was a routine both men enjoyed, and after Bill's death, Stan surely missed the camaraderie. Wherever he was, Bill must have missed it, too.

Stan would later recall what might be seen as their last visit. "About six months after Mr. Smith's death, I was working on a page of type when I heard his voice, asking 'How's it going, Stan?'

"I didn't see anything; I did not actually hear any sound, but it was as though his question was clearly audible in my mind. There was also a warm, friendly feeling.

"I was not frightened, nor upset ... it was as though I was having the usual Tuesday night visit from the man I had worked with for some 20 years."

Stan gave the incident considerable thought. He was sure of his experience and, as Mrs. Smith was now living alone in the second-floor apartment, decided to mention it to her. Stan didn't want the woman to be alarmed, should something similar happen to her.

When Stan told Mrs. Smith about her husband's visit, however, her reaction was unexpected.

"She was neither surprised nor upset," he remembered. Rather, in a very matter-of-fact way, she offered a story of her own.

"Oh, I saw Bill at the head of the apartment stairs about three weeks after he passed on," she said.

Bill Smith was obviously a man reluctant to desert his loved ones — even after they were separated by death.

Tara's Light

One tragic day in 1986, a girl named Tara Chatain, just two weeks shy of her seventeenth birthday, was killed in an automobile accident. Her parents were devastated, believing they would never speak to their beloved daughter again. They were wrong.

The night of the accident, Tara had borrowed the family car and then allowed a younger friend to drive it a few blocks. The boy lost control of the vehicle on a corner, and it careened into a power pole. Tara's neck was broken and she died instantly.

Several days afterward, Tara's father, Frank, decided to visit the accident scene. He parked his car across the street, and spent several minutes in the early morning quiet, grieving for his daughter.

There was a street lamp perched atop the power pole that the car had crashed into, and Frank noticed that its light was dimmer than the neighbouring lights. He assumed it had been damaged by the collision. The light blinked out, and then on again. On impulse, Frank thought, "Is that you, Tara?"

The light suddenly became extremely bright, then returned to its dim state.

Silently, Frank asked his daughter if she was trying to communicate with him. In response, the light flashed from bright to dim several times. Within minutes, a code was established; a bright light for "yes," and a light out for "no." After a brief conversation, including Tara's reassurance that she was happy and well, Frank drove home. He felt certain he had been in contact with his girl. It would not be the last time.

As the family car had been written off after the accident, Frank Chatain and his wife found themselves in the position of needing to shop for a new vehicle; a chore they had very little heart for. It was surprising then, considering their original lack of enthusiasm, that the Chatains ignored every car the salesman presented in their price range, and opted for a larger, more expensive model. They were inexplicably drawn to the vehicle and, strangely, felt actual joy when they made the purchase.

One dark night on the highway between Campbell River and Port Hardy, the Chatains began to understand what attracted them to their new car. It was raining heavily, and Frank was admittedly driving in excess of the speed limit, when suddenly the headlights went off. As he carefully slowed the car, the lights began to blink and, once the vehicle was safely stopped, they became fully bright. On a hunch, remembering Frank's story, Mrs. Chatain asked, "Is that you, Tara?" She was answered by the lights blinking on and off. The Chatains decided to proceed at a slower speed. Within minutes, they came across a hairpin curve which Frank believes he could not have safely negotiated in the rain, at the speed he had been travelling.

Years later, the Chatains had a collection of such experiences. The car's blinking headlights never failed to warn them of a deer on the road ahead, or even a radar trap. When Frank and his wife drove to the airport to pick up their son, the lights flashed excitedly all the way there. They continued to flash on the way home, until the boy finally agreed to say "hello" to his sister.

In author John Robert Colombo's 1991 book, *Mackenzie King's Ghost*, Frank Chatain recalled the many times Tara has communicated with him, and stressed his credibility.

"My wife and I are not stupid and we don't see ghosts all over the place," he wrote. "We are both working, normal people. We have accepted our loss and we are living with it."

It is a loss that is perhaps made a bit more bearable by the comforting knowledge that Tara, in some way, is still with her parents.

"A Warm, Wonderful Feeling"

It is widely believed that departed loved ones are able to come back to guide us in times of distress. A Cumberland woman named Barbara Dawe knows this to be true. In February of 1980, she was nothing, if not distressed.

"I was a twenty-eight-year-old woman with a six-year-old son and a very bad marriage," she wrote. "To fill the gap, I began drinking very heavily and ended up putting myself in the hospital with acute alcoholism."

In the hospital, it was discovered that, aside from the dependency, Barbara had an actual allergy to alcohol. She later learned that the doctors initially predicted her chances of survival were no more than fifteen percent.

After six weeks, Barbara was informed that she required further treatment at another hospital, and would have to be air-lifted there. She felt frightened and alone until the moment she was on the plane. Then, an unusually warm, secure feeling overwhelmed and relaxed her. Her anxiety over the trip disappeared. In fact, the trip *itself* disappeared.

"It seemed as though we took off and then landed, as if there was no flight in between," she recalled.

At the new hospital, Barbara was settled into a semi-private room. On the other side of the curtain was another woman battling alcoholism. Suddenly, although the curtain was drawn, Barbara realised she could see her new room-mate. Stranger still was the fact that she could also see her own body in the hospital bed, as she hovered high above it. She felt terribly cold and alone — but not for long.

"Suddenly my mom was next to me," Barbara remembered, "and I felt so very warm." Although her mother

131

had died in 1979, she seemed intent upon giving her daughter advice.

"She said 'Barbara, how can you do this to your son? He is all you have in this world ... You have to go back and raise him as only you can do'."

Message delivered, the apparition of Barbara's mother disappeared, and Barbara found herself back in bed. She then rang the nurse to inform her of one other bit of information she had collected during her out-of-body experience.

"I told her the lady in the next bed had been drinking, and the nurse went and recovered a mickey of rye from underneath her pillow." The nurse must have wondered how, through a closed curtain, Barbara had seen the woman sneaking drinks.

Bolstered by her mother's visit, Barbara surprised her doctors and recovered. Five years later, she recalled her supernatural experience to her sister, Margo. When the story was finished, Margo remained incredulous, saying, "Well, I'd sure like some proof." Instantly, she got it.

"She had a steel knitting needle in her hands. Suddenly, it broke completely in half. She hadn't been bending or twisting it in any way," Barbara explained, adding, "This was definitely proof enough for her."

In November of 1994, Barbara Dawe's father passed away, following a long illness. At the same time, her new husband was out of work, and ineligible for unemployment insurance. Barbara was missing her beloved father and worried constantly about finances. Christmas looked bleak.

One day, as she stood staring out a window at the falling snow, she began to cry. She was wondering how she would manage to make such a gloomy holiday seem festive when she was suddenly overcome by a great warmth. Barbara was at once comforted, and the words "don't worry" repeated in her mind.

"As it turned out, I didn't need to worry," she later wrote. "My husband's mother gave us $500 so we could have a Christmas. I hope she knows how much it meant to us — words are sometimes not enough."

Barbara's mother-in-law's kind gift set the tone for the entire season. Everyone's mood brightened, and Barbara felt better than she had since her father's death. Possibly, because she suspected both her parents were really very near.

The night that she decorated the tree, Barbara stayed up after everyone else had gone to bed. As she admired the soft glow of the tinsel and brightly coloured bulbs, she asked her mother for a sign. "Let me know if Dad is with you," she said, and immediately, the light at the top of the Christmas tree blinked four times.

In the days that followed, Barbara's husband fitted the tree-top ornament with different bulbs, but to no avail. "All

Barbara Dawe with her parents, in 1971. Today, though both her mother and father have died, Barbara feels their caring presence often.

(Photograph courtesy of Barbara Dawe)

through the season, the tree blinked sporadically," Barbara remembered, "and we had one of the best Christmases ever."

Today, Barbara still feels the nearly constant presence of her loving parents. To let her know they are there, the television will turn off on its own. Once, at Barbara's request, a scented candle began burning two flames, then returned to one the instant she left the room. And another time, a slipper that Barbara playfully threw at her husband stopped in mid-air, then smacked him directly on the forehead. "Watch out," she likes to tease her husband now, "or my mom will get you!"

Barbara sees all the phenomena as "very special events" in her life. To this day, she is not sure how to explain them, but feels loved and protected when they occur. Every time that "warm, wonderful feeling" returns, she knows her mom and dad are still nearby; still taking care of her, as they did in life.

The Heirloom

When a spirit returns with a message, its reasons aren't necessarily clear. To this day, the teller of this next tale is not sure why a certain tablecloth was so important to her ghost.

When Pam Fletcher remembers the home of her youth, the images are vivid and inviting.

"I will never forget the fireplace, with the logs snapping and crackling on a cold winter's night ... I would spend the evening listening to records or the radio ... Later, tea would be served with fruit cake and lemon tarts. [In the summer] I had days of playing tennis and swimming in the lakes to look forward to ... there were also loganberries to be picked at a nearby farm."

Given this idyllic description, it is difficult to imagine an experience so unsettling that, for years, Pam would refuse to be in the seemingly cheerful house alone. Yet, she wrote of one, in the summer of 1995 — a full seventy years after the fact.

"Sunshine flooded the kitchen of our home on the hill, that July day," she reminisced. "School was out, summer holidays were starting ... This year my dreams were of a black bathing suit with a white belt. As I leaned against our big kitchen window, gazing at the lovely open fields and the woods beyond them, my thoughts were certainly not on ghosts or unseen spectres."

Yet, suddenly, without warning, Pam's pleasant daydreams were interrupted. "I felt very odd," she explained. "My hair felt like it was rising on the back of my neck. I have never felt so scared ... something or someone was in that room with me! My fright rooted me to the spot. The presence was so strong, I was convinced this unseen being was going to touch my shoulder!"

This knowledge was enough to break her panic-induced paralysis. Screaming, she ran from the house — and never again would she let herself be alone in it.

As for whom the presence might have been, Pam had only one theory. Shortly before her unsettling experience, a close friend named Mrs. Colt had died. Mrs. Colt was dearly missed by every member of Pam's family and, following her funeral, the woman's son had given each one of them a gift of one of her possessions. Pam received a hand-made lace tablecloth; an heirloom, the son said.

After receiving the tablecloth, Pam was plagued with recurring nightmares. "Mrs. Colt would appear in this dream and demand her tablecloth back. I never knew whether I gave it to her, as I would wake up in a cold sweat before my dream ended."

Interestingly, the nightmares ended, following Pam's frightening experience in the kitchen. Perhaps the presence Pam felt was Mrs. Colt, making one final, tremendous effort to reclaim her cloth.

"Or maybe she forgot about me," Pam theorizes, "after I gave the heirloom tablecloth away to a church bazaar."

There's no way to be sure — but it would be interesting to know where that lace cloth is today, and whether its present owner dreams of a strange woman, demanding its return.

Norman Taylor's Message

*The following story raises an interesting question: Was this a
simple case of a ghost passing along information, or is it proof of
spiritual intervention in the world of the living?*

There are many stories of messages from the spirit world being
delivered via Ouija board — but few are as compelling as this
tale from just outside Victoria.

 The story goes that a family had begun using the Ouija as
a regular form of entertainment. For several sessions in a row, the
same spirit appeared to converse with them: a fellow who called
himself "Norman Taylor."

 Norman Taylor delighted the family and their friends by
revealing "wonderful things about themselves." T.W. Paterson
wrote about the family's experience in the January 26, 1969
edition of the *Daily Colonist*.

> For one young lady he had a special message: He
> would send a friend to her. She would know him
> when he placed a signet ring on her finger. The
> lass had blushed becomingly, all had made merry
> of the incident and the night ended as usual.

According to Paterson's report, three years went by and
the Ouija board and Norman Taylor had been forgotten, when
the young woman fell in love with a fellow who was new to
Victoria. One day, the man proposed marriage and she
accepted.

 As he slipped a ring on her finger, the woman suddenly
remembered her Ouija experience. Paterson wrote that the
woman exclaimed, "Why, that must be the ring Norman Taylor
told me about!"

The woman's fiancé appeared shocked. How, he asked, had she known the fellow he went to school with in Australia? He found it particularly puzzling, considering that his friend Norman had died — years before, and thousands of miles away.

The woman had no answer; only a startlingly accurate message from someone who had been her fiance's friend in life — and her own, after death.

CHAPTER EIGHT

Children and the Paranormal

A woman was asked by her nine-year-old daughter what an aura was. She tried to explain the halos of light, colour, and energy that are believed to emanate from each living thing, and the girl casually replied, "Oh, those. Everybody had those until grade one."

Among people who believe in the existence of ghosts, it is generally accepted that children tend to be more sensitive to the phenomena than are adults. The commonly held theory is that a young child's innocence and lack of conditioning allows him to accept what he sees. "Children ... are less skeptical," writes Some Canadian Ghosts *(1973) author Sheila Hervey; "less apt to criticize the evidence of their own senses."*

According to University of Regina parapsychologist Dr. Buddy Wynn, "Children do not yet hold socialized beliefs of what is and isn't possible. They don't have the blinders on."

It makes one wonder how many "invisible friends" are perhaps more than the product of a child's active imagination ...

Kukin and Frindon

Children with few playmates are often creative enough to invent their own. When little Chris Dixon was only two years old, this is exactly what his parents thought he was doing.

"He one day announced that he had two new friends," Chris's father, Dave Dixon, recalled. "He called them 'Kukin and Frindon.'"

Dave and his wife, Patricia, thought nothing of it at the time, but years later, would view the arrival of Kukin and Frindon as the beginning of one of the strangest experiences of their lives.

Chris Dixon with his young sister, Jennifer, in the bedroom where "Kukin and Frindon" would visit.
(Photograph courtesy of Dave and Patricia Dixon)

The Dixons had rented the same, small, two-bedroom bungalow on the outskirts of North Burnaby since before Chris was born. It was, according to Dave Dixon, "so old that a friend of my mother's who had lived in Burnaby all of her life could remember a woman who lived in the house giving birth to her fourteenth child. This was in the 1930s, and the house was *old* then!"

Like most homes its age, the Dixon residence was poorly insulated and could be a bit chilly in the winter months. Still, there was no explaining how the smaller of the two bedrooms, which opened directly off the living room, was always colder than the rest of the house. This odd difference in temperature and the eerie sensation of being watched — a feeling so strong that Patricia would often rouse Dave in the middle of the night, insisting that someone must have broken in — were the only indications of unusual events to come.

Chris Dixon was born soon after his parents moved into the Burnaby house and, once he was old enough, the small bedroom became his. This is where Kukin and Frindon, his "invisible playmates," came to visit.

As the months passed, Chris's accounts of these visits became increasingly detailed. The stories soon seemed too sophisticated for a toddler to invent, and the Dixons began to wonder if their son's imaginary friends were really so imaginary.

According to Chris, Kukin and Frindon only appeared at night, when everyone else was asleep. They would arrive, he said, by walking through the wall.

"Bear in mind," wrote Dave Dixon, "that Chris had no access to older children or Sci-Fi television programs."

Concerned, Dave and Patricia began to question Chris more closely. They asked their son where Kukin and Frindon came from. Chris replied, "From the other side."

"The other side of what?" the Dixons pressed.

"The river," he answered. There was no river where the family lived.

What alarmed Dave and Patricia most, however, was Chris's comment that Kukin and Frindon often wanted him to return with them, when they left.

"At this point," wrote Patricia, "we felt that Chris might be in some danger and advised him never to go with them. We repeated this warning time and again."

The visits continued, three or four nights a week. They ended only when Chris was three years old and the Dixons moved away.

"After the first night at our new house, we asked Chris what his friends thought of his new bedroom. Chris told us that his friends had to stay at the old house, they couldn't leave. Chris never spoke of them again."

Which is not to say the Dixons never *heard* of them, again.

When Dave and Patricia moved out of the Burnaby house, two young men, who were their friends, took over the lease. The arrangement lasted only two months.

The fellow who moved into Chris's old bedroom found sleeping there nearly impossible. He would awaken at night, certain that he was being watched. The feeling was so powerful that he began avoiding the room, altogether, and slept on a recliner in the living room. But, according to Dave Dixon, this didn't solve the problem.

"One night he awoke with a stronger premonition than usual, and he looked across the darkened room to the doorway leading to the small bedroom. In that instant, he believed he saw two shadowy figures standing just inside the bedroom. He came fully awake and dashed into the bedroom, thinking kids had maybe come in through the window. He found no signs of any intrusion."

The next day, he and his room-mate decided to move out. Apparently, they felt no need for the "imaginary" playmates that entertained Chris for a year.

It is interesting to note that the young man could not have been influenced by the Dixon's own story. According to Dave, they never told anyone about their son's experience.

To this day, however, the Dixons are curious about the old bungalow and its shadowy inhabitants, Kukin and Frindon. They speculate that perhaps there was a connection to the story of the woman with fourteen children, but cannot be sure.

"Who the two children were, or why they continue to haunt the little house in Burnaby, we will never know," wrote Dave.

What they do know is this: the house still stands, and someone lives there today. And very likely, Kukin and Frindon continue to make their night-time visits.

*****

Patricia Dixon has something unique in common with her son. When she was a young child, in Burnaby, she lived with a ghost of her own. That story, in her own words, follows.

Phantom Footsteps

"When I was a child, I lived with my parents and three sisters in an old house owned by the Catholic parish. Upstairs, my sisters and I shared two bedrooms; one at each end of the house separated by a long hallway.

"Soon after moving in, we began to hear what sounded like footsteps walking in the attic, from one bedroom across to the other. The footsteps would pause above each room before returning to the other. My sisters and I would shout at one another, 'He's coming your way!' as he made his way back and forth.

This house on Triumph Street, in Burnaby, was demolished to make way for a Catholic school playground. Patricia Dixon grew up there, listening to the eerie sounds of disembodied footsteps.
(Photograph courtesy of Dave and Patricia Dixon)

"Our parents never heard our night-time visitor. When we described the sounds to them, they said it must have been a pigeon. However, to my sisters and I, who heard it, there was no mistaking the distinctive sound of heavy footfalls as the 'phantom' paced the attic floor, night after night!"

144

The McIntyre Mystery

In a condominium on Vancouver's Premier Street, in the mid-1970s, objects flew, doors slammed, and mysterious voices could be heard murmuring, late at night. Who was responsible? According to a little boy named Jason McIntyre, it was all the work of a ghost named "Johnny." Johnny had been making nightly visits for three years — most of young Jason's life.

When the activity became public knowledge, it was enough to prompt an exorcism, a clinical investigation, warring newspaper accounts two days before Christmas, and several opposing theories regarding its origin. Rarely had there been so much phenomena to investigate and so little agreement regarding its interpretation.

According to Jason's mother, twenty-one-year-old Avril McIntyre, the strange activity started when her son was only four months old.

"I found him one night sitting up in bed roaring with laughter — he was completely exhausted," she told Philip Mills in the December 23, 1976, *Province*. It was the first of many strange things to happen in the McIntyre household.

As Jason grew older, the activity surrounding him grew more frequent and more intense. When the boy was two years old, his mother entered his room one night and found it in chaos. Sheets and blankets were torn; toys, destroyed. The sturdy legs on Jason's bed had been broken off. Oddly, Avril McIntyre heard nothing, while the destruction took place.

By the summer of 1976, Jason was three years old, and unexplainable occurrences in the McIntyre home were at an all-time high. Cupboard doors and drawers began to crash open, without warning. Ornaments and small kitchen appliances flew through the air. The condominium's heavy fire door would open, unassisted, and swag lamps swayed dramatically when there was no hint of a breeze. Jason had an explanation for everything: he claimed "Johnny did it."

According to Jason, Johnny was over six feet tall and blonde. He said the man wore buckskins, "like Dan'l Boon," and visited every single night.

Wanting to know who her son's nocturnal guest was, Avril McIntyre invested in a Ouija board and began to experiment with it. She was frightened away from the experiment, however, when the planchette began to move on its own.

"I phoned a Catholic priest and he told me to burn the board," she told the *Province*. "We needed two cans of fuel in the end, the board just wouldn't burn."

Avril McIntyre's attempt to contact the spirit had failed — but according to a clinical psychologist, Dr. Lee Pulos, it wasn't a ghost that the McIntyres were dealing with, anyway. It was the power of the mind.

Psychokinesis is the term used to describe the invisible influence of mind over matter. People who have the ability are able to use non-physical force to move or break objects, bend metal, and even cause materializations. Levitations, healings, and many "hauntings" have been explained using the theory of psychokinesis, or "PK." It is believed that the power can be used consciously or unconsciously — and can therefore leave even the person who is causing the phenomena confused and frightened.

Dr. Pulos believed this to be the case with the McIntyres. He theorized that the paranormal activity was the result of Jason's unleashed talent, and that the boy had created an imaginary character called "Johnny" to explain something he did not understand. Dr. George Owen, a mathematical physicist and head of the Toronto Society for Psychical Research, backed Pulos up in the December 23, 1976 edition of the *Vancouver Sun*. "There are endless reports of this [phenomena] happening," he said. "It has been witnessed and documented on many occasions and it has nothing at all to do with spirits or ghosts."

But there were those who would not agree. Isabel Corlett, vice-president of the Vancouver Psychic Society, believed that Johnny was a ghost; likely the spirit of someone not resting well in the nearby native burial ground. The Burrard Indian Band chief concurred there was a burial ground in the area of the McIntyre home.

In early December of 1976, Isabel Corlett and an "Indian princess" visited the McIntyres, intending to conduct a sort of spiritual clearing. "I felt very eerie, but then we swished cedar branches around the home and the atmosphere improved," she told the *Province* later that month. Still, there was no sure way of knowing whether Johnny was a ghost or an imaginative product of Jason's mind.

Even Avril McIntyre's friends, who were witness to much of the phenomena, seemed non-committal. Eileen Foster, a neighbour, claimed to have seen an empty vase unexplainably refill itself with murky water, although Mrs. McIntyre emptied it repeatedly — yet seemed unconvinced that anything paranormal was happening in the house. "I can't say yes and I can't say no," was her quote in the December 23, 1976 edition of the *Province*.

Other people had experienced the sensation of being touched, heard growling noises, and seen pictures moving and lamp shades spinning. While they trusted their senses, they may have been hesitant to interpret what they had witnessed. Were the McIntyres dealing with a ghost, or did Jason possess psychokinetic powers?

Judging by her own contradictory newspaper quotes, it would seem even Avril McIntyre couldn't form an opinion. "Ghosts I won't buy, but I'm willing to accept psychokinesis," she told the *Vancouver Sun* on December 23, 1976. Yet, in the same article, she claimed to have sensed "Johnny's" presence and even heard his voice, in her home. "I'm sure it wasn't Jason talking," McIntyre said. "There's no way he could get his voice down that low."

McIntyre also told the *Vancouver Sun* that she felt "reassured" by the presence in her home, then contradicted herself on the same day in the *Province*, when she talked about hiding under her bedcovers when she would hear the ghost. "What a terrible mother I must sound," she said, "but it's really scary."

Frightening or reassuring; spiritual activity or psychokinetic energy; invention or fact? Twenty years later, there's only one thing known for certain: the strange stories surrounding one little boy and his "invisible friend" were fascinating enough to warrant news coverage of a story typically reserved for Hallowe'en on the day before Christmas Eve.

Whatever else "Johnny" may have been, he was good copy.

Caitie's Friend

It was 1990 when Janice and Ed Clapp decided to leave their home in Ottawa "in pursuit of a calmer existence" on Vancouver Island. With their two-year-old daughter Caitie in tow, they travelled across the country in a van searching for the perfect, charming house to turn into a bed-and-breakfast venture. They found that house on Windemere Avenue in Cumberland. Whether they found the calmer existence is up for debate.

"The house was eighty-five years old and in dire need of repair," Janice recalled. Still, the Clapps were excited by the home's potential. It boasted 3,500 square feet, five bedrooms, and a distinctive history, having been originally owned by one of the founding members of Cumberland Hospital, a doctor by the name of McNaughton. The home had charm, albeit hidden by years of neglect, and in August of 1990, Janice and Ed began working to bring it out.

Janice Clapp, with Caitie, doing renovations to the house.
(Photograph courtesy of Janice Clapp)

Part of the extensive renovation process was research. As the Clapps wished "not to alter, but enhance" the Windemere Avenue house, they asked dozens of questions about its original state. By December 16, when they invited the public to an opening celebration, the home looked as grand as the day Dr. McNaughton moved into it with his family. To those who attended the open house, it would seem the past had come alive. Years later, Janice would wonder if, in fact, it hadn't.

The bed and breakfast on Windemere Avenue in Cumberland.
(Photograph courtesy of Janice Clapp)

Little Caitie Clapp was two and a half when the family moved into the restored home. It is an age when children are typically imaginative, so her parents were not surprised when she began talking about the "ghost" of a little girl in the corner of her bedroom. They dismissed it as a phase Caitie was going through, yet with each passing night, she offered more details about the spectre.

Dr. McNaughton was the original owner of the house. His young daughter, who died of Spanish Influenza in 1918, may have been Caitie's "ghost."

(Photograph courtesy of Janice Clapp)

"Go away ghosts and goblins, witches, get out," became a bedtime ritual with Caitie, as her parents made a great business of shooing unwanted paranormal types out of her room.

"This took place every night for about three months," wrote Janice, "when we finally said she had to start the shooing on her own — and she did." This passing of responsibility did nothing to discourage Caitie's fantasy, however. The ghost, she claimed, was still there.

It was around this time that the Clapps received a telephone call informing them that one of Dr. McNaughton's daughters was coming to Cumberland and would love to see her old home restored. Anxious to see the woman's reaction to their work, Janice and Ed invited her for a tour. It would prove interesting for everyone involved.

Janice and Ed engaged Dr. McNaughton's daughter with the details of their extensive renovation. She entertained them with stories of their home's past. But it was one casual remark, made after touring the bedrooms, that captured Janice's attention.

"She commented on how her sister had, in fact, died of influenza ... and that although her dad was a doctor, there was nothing he could do."

Janice was intrigued. Could Caitie's ghost be the little McNaughton girl who was lost to the Spanish Influenza epidemic of 1918? Suddenly, other odd occurrences seemed to bear greater consideration. "I had often heard noises, like footsteps, from the top floor when we were downstairs," Janice remembered, "but passed them off as my imagination."

It is natural to wonder why, after more than sixty years, the spirit of the young girl chose to materialize for the Clapps — but there are theories that make sense of the situation.

Renovations have often been reported to stir up paranormal activity; sometimes because the ghost takes offense at extensive changes, but more likely, in this case, because its former environment has been lovingly recreated. The other probable explanation is that Caitie, at her sensitive young age, acted as a sort of catalyst, encouraging the phenomena. This supports Janice Clapp's own conclusions.

"To this day I often wonder if [the ghost of the little girl] was indeed some lost soul who left Windemere Avenue back during the influenza epidemic and came back to find a friend in Caitie," she wrote, also wondering if, had they stayed in the house, the ghost "would have made her presence more evident."

There is no way of knowing. Ed and Janice Clapp sold their beloved bed and breakfast in 1991, and the house has again undergone major changes.

Does the little McNaughton girl approve? Does she visit? Only the current tenants know for sure.

Quiet Companion

In early 1996, Brenda Hatton, of New Hazelton, took the time to write down an interesting incident that took place a few years ago in her part of the province:

A five-year-old girl was talking to her grandmother about the house the girl's family had moved into, just west of Hazelton. The youngster's new bedroom seemed to have a special and unusual feature — an old lady who would enter the room, late at night.

Humouring the child, her grandmother asked, "Oh, and what does she do?"

"Nothing," the girl replied. "She just sits and knits."

When the grandmother asked if the old lady ever spoke, the girl seemed somewhat horrified. "No, of course not!" was the indignant reply.

Amused by the imaginative story, the grandmother later relayed it to the child's mother. Upon hearing it, however, the mother seemed more surprised than entertained.

She explained that before she and her husband had purchased the home, its previous owner had passed away, there. She was an old woman who was in the habit of spending many hours in her bedroom, knitting. Interestingly, her bedroom was the one the little girl came to occupy.

Because it was trivial information which never came up in conversation, the child couldn't have known this. And since she was too young to understand that it was decidedly unusual to have a stranger knitting in her bedroom, she wasn't alarmed.

She simply accepted the nightly visits.

*****

As children grow older and adopt a more logical, analytical way of thinking, the ability to sense what adults cannot usually fades.

For a few, however, the turbulent emotions of adolescence seem to attract, or have a catalytic influence on, spiritual energy. The teenage years, for these people, can be even stranger than expected.

An Eventful Year

Dawn Scott, of Nelson, British Columbia, was witness to a paranormal event involving her father and her boyfriend in the chapter 7 story, "The Gift." Prior to that, however, Dawn had a couple of experiences of her own — both taking place when she was fourteen years of age.

On the first occasion, Dawn was washing her hair in the kitchen sink, when she felt the sensitive skin on the back of her neck begin to prickle. The girl was suddenly certain that someone was behind her, watching her intently, yet she knew that couldn't be. The only other person in the house was Dawn's mother, and Dawn could hear her in the bathroom, preparing to go out for the evening.

The kitchen window above the sink provided a reflection of the room and, carefully, Dawn checked it. There appeared to be no one behind her, yet the uncomfortable feeling refused to go away.

"Finally," reported Dawn, "I looked behind me as fast as I could, [trying] to catch something I couldn't see in the reflection. I caught something, all right."

What Dawn saw, when she spun around, was not a person, however — but a bizarre spectacle.

"The belt my mother had hung over the kitchen chair was actually lifting itself up and down."

Dawn called frantically for her mother to come and see the strange sight, but the moment the older woman walked out of the bathroom, the belt draped itself calmly over the chair back and stayed there.

The second event might initially have been written off as the side effect of an illness, for it happened when Dawn was suffering from a serious case of influenza.

"My temperature was 105 degrees," she wrote, adding logically, "of course I was delirious." Dawn was even aware of her delirium at the time and, so, dismissed a number of things she "saw" as the result of her illness.

"I saw the devil's head come out of our living room floor. I saw a mother cat and her kittens being fed on our rocking chair. I saw several things that my mind kept telling me were my imagination, because I was sick," recalled Dawn. "Then, I saw this huge lady with a raincoat and a big flimsy rain hat on her head, fall to the ground right before my eyes."

All these images would have been forgotten in time, were it not for a certain photograph taken of Dawn, shortly thereafter. In it, reflected in a window, it is easy to see two figures standing side by side.

"However faded they may be," said Dawn, in amazement, "I can still make out a raincoat and a flimsy-looking rain hat on a fat woman's body."

Melinda's Stories

"I wish to share with you some of my experiences that I can't explain, but I hope that my young age doesn't affect my credibility."

So began a letter from fifteen-year-old Melinda Medland, detailing several strange incidents that took place near Trail, British Columbia. Her sincere, matter-of-fact delivery certainly was not discredited by her age — and, interestingly, the very fact of her youth may be the reason she had these experiences, at all.

"My first experience with the unexplained was about two years ago, at the end of grade eight." It may be worth noting that this would have been the beginning of Melinda's teenage years.

Melinda and a friend named Ashley were spending the night at the home of a third friend, Lisa. Amateur séances have always been a slumber party standard, and Melinda and her friends decided to try one.

"We found a large rectangular mirror and put it on the floor and then placed ourselves around it," she wrote. "We dimmed the lights and held hands."

As Melinda looked down into the mirror, she noticed the necklace she was wearing, a St. Christopher's medallion, swinging gently back and forth. The pendant would catch the low lights, every few seconds, as the girls tried to communicate with the spirit world.

A few minutes later, the three friends decided that, as they were getting no response, their séance was a failure. They abandoned the idea, but before Melinda stood up, she instinctively reached for her necklace. It was gone.

"I checked all my clothes and my body, as well as the surrounding area, but it was nowhere to be found. I have not seen my necklace since that night."

In the months to follow, that house would be the site of numerous strange happenings. Knives sitting on the kitchen counter top would suddenly clatter to the floor, and lights would often flicker on and off. Melinda and Lisa were alone in the house, one day, when they distinctly heard someone run down all the stairs from the second floor to the basement. A television that was turned off before everyone fell asleep came to life by itself in the middle of the night, and mysterious knocking noises were often heard.

"We think the house is haunted," wrote Melinda; a reasonable assumption, given all that has happened there. However, the young woman's paranormal experiences have not been restricted to her friend's home. One night, in her own bedroom, she had just gone to bed and shut off the light when she heard a strange noise.

"[It] sounded like a poster rustling," Melinda recalled. "I turned on my lamp to see if my poster had fallen from the back of my door. It had not, and didn't appear to be moving at all."

It couldn't have been the wind; Melinda noted that both her door and window were securely shut. She decided to dismiss the incident, and turned the light off, once more. Seconds later, she was again hearing noises in the dark.

"I heard a knocking, right by my head, in the corner of the wall. I felt uneasy, but was then swept over with a sense of security and calm. Then, it felt like someone depressed my pillow slightly and was stroking my hair gently. I'm not sure why, but I smiled and fell asleep."

Is Melinda a natural "sensitive," gifted for life, or will these incidents be limited to her adolescence? Had she been ten years older, would the gentle ghost in her bedroom have been able to communicate with her?

As with all young people who experience the paranormal, it's a question that will only be answered with time.

The See-Through Man

If children are to show any extra awareness of the paranormal, it is usually during the innocence of the preschool years or the turbulence of adolescence. It can happen in the years between, however, and when it does, the child suffers a unique predicament — being old enough to know what they are witnessing, but far too young to be credible to adults or have any control over the situation.

The following is an interesting tale of a young boy in such a position.

When Graham Mitchell (a pseudonym) was eight years old, his family moved to an acreage outside Parksville on Vancouver Island. His parents, brothers, and sister were enthusiastic about their spacious new farmhouse and the prospect of country life. Graham was not.

"They loved it. I *hated* it," he stressed, recalling the place where he spent most of his childhood.

It wasn't only that Graham missed the city and was unaccustomed to the relative isolation that twenty acres provided. It was the intuitive impression he got from the house.

"It was horrible. I always felt horrible feelings there."

At first, if he ever took a moment to analyze his incessant dark mood, Graham likely attributed it to being unhappy about the move. But when the family had lived there one year, the boy had an experience which led him to believe that the new house, itself, might be to blame.

When it happened, Graham's father was away, working in Vancouver. His brothers and sister were upstairs, asleep. Graham and his mother were alone on the main floor of the house; she, in the kitchen, he, in his room, preparing for bed.

Graham's bedroom was directly opposite his parents' room. As he put on his pyjamas, he happened to look across the hall. He was shocked to see that there, beside his mother's dresser, stood a young man with dark hair and a moustache, looking back at him. Graham froze. Was it an intruder? Should he yell for his mother? Or could this man be a legitimate visitor?

He stared at the man for many long moments before Graham realized one all-important fact: he could see through him. "It was like he was constructed out of smoke," Graham would later recall. The stranger was clearly defined, but had an eerie, slightly transparent quality.

Graham was stunned. Not knowing what to do, he broke away from the ghost's gaze and hurried to the warmth of the kitchen, where his mother was. Once there, he said nothing, but sat down and waited. He knew his mother would go into her bedroom in a few minutes, and if she saw the see-through man too, it would mean he wasn't imagining things.

Before long, Graham's mother went to her bedroom. Time passed. Nothing happened. She had obviously found the room to be empty, and so, Graham began to question what he had seen.

The fact was, he rather wanted the ghost to be a figment of his imagination. Graham was nine years old when he met the apparition; his family would live on the acreage for another seven years. He later admitted that that time would have been unbearable, had he acknowledged he was living with a spectre. And, as a child, he could do nothing to change the situation.

"If I — as a kid, especially — admitted there was a ghost, how could I put up with living there? I'm a *kid*, I can't pick up and leave."

It was as good a reason as any to deny the experience, and when other strange things began to happen, Graham dealt with them similarly.

"There would be times when I was home, alone, watching television — and, in the kitchen, I could hear drawers sliding open and utensils being rattled. But, of course, I would never admit it might be a ghost, or that there was someone there. So I would tell myself that it was the cats. But I *know* that's physically impossible."

Graham never felt comfortable in the house. During the day, he sensed a vague, constant threat; at night, he was plagued by a recurring nightmare of being alone at home, with the rooms stripped bare of furnishings, and seeing a face leer in the window.

It wasn't until his teen years, however, that he discovered a possible cause of the haunting. Apparently, the people who had built the house had a son who was killed in a logging accident. He had been a young man, and it was a young man Graham had seen in the bedroom that night. He wondered if there was a connection, and even thought of going to the local newspaper office to see if they had published a photograph with their coverage of the accident. In the end, he did nothing. Graham remembered the man's face so vividly that it would be easy to make a positive identification, and while he still lived in the house, he wanted no confirmation of his suspicions.

In 1988, the Mitchells moved to Vancouver. The relief Graham felt no doubt saw him through his final night in the farmhouse, a night which almost literally recreated the nightmare he had experienced for years.

"Everyone except my mother and myself had left for Vancouver," he remembered. "We were going to do the final clean-up and take all the animals over the next day. So ... the house was empty, all the furniture was gone, just like in the dream, and we were the only ones there. That last night was the hardest night of my life. I was just on a mattress, on the floor — and, the whole night, I couldn't sleep unless I had a fire poker in my hand. I was so sure I would look up at the window and see someone staring in at me."

In the morning, Graham left the acreage — and, with it, his eight-year fear of the mysterious "see-through man." But the story was not quite over.

The people who occupied the farmhouse after the Mitchell family moved away had a dog who would unfailingly bark to announce the arrival of any stranger on the property. But one day, the woman was out in the yard with the dog, when she noticed something strange.

There was a dark-haired young man with a moustache standing at the edge of the drive, staring in her direction. He did nothing, he said nothing, and after a few moments he simply turned around and walked into the woods. Aside from the man's behaviour, she later said, the decidedly odd thing about the whole situation was that the dog never barked. In fact, it didn't even seem to notice anyone there. When Graham heard this story, he felt chilled.

"For the first time, [my story] was substantiated. Someone else had seen something strange, there."

Graham would never see or hear of the silent, spectral, dark-haired young man again. He would never again feel uneasy in his own home, hear unexplainable noises when he knew he was alone, or experience the recurring nightmare. And that was just fine.

Eight years had been quite enough.

CHAPTER NINE

Apparitions

Since "seeing is believing," it is no wonder that apparitions make the liveliest and most credible ghost stories. While other phenomena may be explained in a variety of ways, both normal and paranormal, the apparition is, by nature, difficult to dismiss or rationalize.

It is possible to explain one-time incidents as invention, imagination, or a hallucination caused by telepathic or physical influences — but what of collective apparitions, where many people see the same thing at the same time? Or — perhaps even more convincing — recurrent, localized apparitions, where the ghost is seen by a number of people over a number of years? In this scenario, the witnesses are usually unaware of each other's experiences (and even each other), so collaborating on a story or receiving identical telepathic messages is impossible.

Certain ghosts, referred to by parapsychologists as "veridical apparitions," are most interesting because they can be corroborated by fact. These are the cases where the witness of an apparition is in possession of some knowledge they would not likely have, naturally. Never having met the deceased, they can pick them out of a photo line-up. Not knowing what events transpired at the site, they can describe a scene which is later confirmed. Being unaware of the dead person's habits and behaviour, they can nonetheless describe them in detail.

Given these considerations, it is reasonable to theorize that an apparition may be either a visual impression left on the *fabric of time and place (particularly where the ghost engages in the same behaviour repeatedly, or the scene is one with strong emotional impact, usually violent), or some surviving aspect of a person, following death (particularly where the ghost seems aware of its surroundings and even interacts with the living).*

Apparitions are the most rare form of haunting, but still, British Columbia has its fair share. Many have been discussed in previous chapters; now, here are a handful more.

The Woman
Through the Wall

Ghost stories are filled with images of spirits acting in ways that are physically impossible for the living. They walk effortlessly through walls and furniture. They skim over water, as if it was a solid surface. Even witnesses, themselves, are no obstacle; ghosts have been known to pass right through them.

It is often assumed that spirits are acting consciously, using their lack of physical limitation to overcome the environment. It is more probable, however, that the actions are very unconscious, and the reasons more grounded in the mundane.

If one theorizes that a ghost is somehow trapped in the past, it is reasonable to assume that they are also trapped in the landscape of that time. For example, a ghost who appears to float upward may simply be ascending a staircase which once existed, but has since been lost to renovations. The spectre who walks inches above the ground may be treading soil now eroded away.

A few years ago, in Greenwood, a man named Glen Drinkwater had an experience that would tend to support this theory.

Glen's home was one of Greenwood's older buildings, and it had a bit of a sordid history. The house was known to have once been a brothel, but times had changed, the girls moved out, renovations were done, and the place had long been a private residence.

One night, however, a bit of the past seemed to seep through. Glen was lying in bed when he heard the faint sound of laughter. Thinking someone was just outside the house, he rose to investigate. What he saw was the figure of a woman. She appeared before him for mere seconds before walking directly toward, and then through, the wall.

The strange sight made such an strong impression, Glen remembered the exact spot on the wall where the woman had faded away. Some time later, he was reinsulating the house and needed to break through the wall at that particular point. He would always remember what he discovered.

"Right where the figure had disappeared," recalled Glen, "there were two beams. [It was obviously] where a door used to be."

Another renovation to the house had entailed the removal of the entire third storey, and the ghosts didn't seem to be aware of that change, either. Footsteps were frequently heard on the roof, where a floor once lay.

By 1994, Glen Drinkwater had moved out of the home, and the Stephensons arrived from Victoria. They had no knowledge of what Glen witnessed in the house, but after moving in, began to have strange experiences of their own.

Zoe Stephenson also heard the frequent and mysterious sounds of someone walking around on her flat-topped roof. And, although she never saw the woman who walked through walls, she did have a strong aversion to one of the upstairs rooms.

"I couldn't really explain what I felt," wrote Zoe, "but I knew that I was uncomfortable when I went near that door or into that particular room."

The feelings were so strong that a visiting family member sensed them, and suggested a solution. Being a woman of strong religious conviction, she felt that a prayer and anointing of the house might have a cleansing effect. Zoe agreed to try it.

"When we entered the room, we became very cold and broke out in goose bumps, even though it was the end of July and very hot. She was obviously much stronger in her faith than I was, as immediately after the prayer, the cold spirit left her, but transferred to me. It was as though a cool breeze had encircled my shoulders. Another prayer was said, this time with more authority, and although I had been skeptical of what was being done, I felt the cold spirit unwind from me."

The women completed the ceremony by placing the sign of the cross over every doorway, then returned to the main floor, feeling confident that their efforts had been effective. Two years later, Zoe still held that confidence.

"Whatever the cold spirit was ... it definitely couldn't stay, and it hasn't returned," she wrote.

The only other strange event took place immediately following the "spiritual cleansing" that Zoe and her companion performed.

"My fourteen-year-old son came home, and we told him what we had done. He went up to his room to look at where the crosses had been placed, and then became somewhat alarmed. The cross above his bedroom door had dissolved into a red smudge, almost as though it had bled."

Zoe replaced the smudged symbol with a fresh one, and nothing further happened — but by this time, the young man had convinced himself that someone had died in his room.

"My son preferred to sleep downstairs for a few days," Zoe concluded.

All things considered, few would blame him.

The Appearance of "Abe"

Apparitions are not all created equal. According to those who have seen them, they range from vague, transparent shapes constructed of light or shadow, to ghosts of such realistic appearance that they can be mistaken for living people.

When Denise Taft of Quesnel was thirteen years old, she was visited by a spirit whose features were so vivid, the details are still clear in her mind.

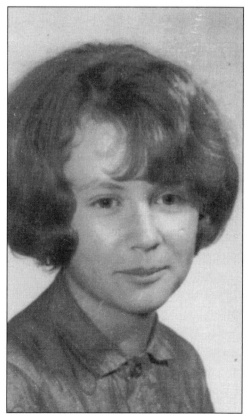

Denise Taft, in 1964; the year she was awakened by an apparition.
(Photograph courtesy of Denise Taft)

It was 1964, and Denise's family was living in Port Moody. She awoke suddenly, one night, to see a man standing beside her bed, looking down at her. The image was one she would never forget.

"He had a long skinny face, sunken eyes, high cheekbones, sunken cheeks and a large pointed nose," she would recall more than thirty years later. The man's costume was equally memorable. He must have appeared sombre and somewhat eccentric in his coal-black suit, top-hat, and matching cape, made dramatically complete by its red satin lining.

Denise was shocked and frightened to find this stranger leaning over her. She stared at him, wondering what he might do next. What he *did* do next was fascinating.

The mysterious man in black was floating.

"He floated toward the ceiling," wrote Denise. "His arms were at his side with his palms facing frontwards. He kept looking at me as he floated upwards."

When the man reached the bedroom ceiling, he did not stop, but drifted effortlessly through it. Just before he disappeared, Denise saw a bright light shining on the ghost's face, allowing her to see his features even more clearly.

"I remember thinking later that he looked like Abe Lincoln," she recalled.

Denise remained wide awake, but the rest of the night was mercifully uneventful. To her knowledge, the visitor never did return, but she thinks of the experience frequently.

"I often wonder what it was supposed to mean," she wrote, many years later.

Perhaps, nothing. But that doesn't make the floating stranger any less intriguing.

The Intruder

"In the year 1965, my husband and our three children moved to a house we bought in Burnaby, BC, on Georgia Street."

Ann Nelson remembers countless details about that house; it was a place she adored.

"We had a peach tree that grew peaches the size of grapefruit just outside of our kitchen window," she recalled. "The yard was nice and big; lots of space for our children to play in. We had nice neighbours ... Everything was great. We loved our house very much."

Why, then, did the Nelson family live there for only a brief period before deciding to sell the house and move to another Burnaby neighbourhood? It began simply enough, with a child reporting what was probably believed to be a dream.

"Our son Jim got up one morning and said 'Mom, there was something in my bedroom last night,'" Ann wrote. The boy told his mother that he was sure something was hiding in his clothes closet, and that he had felt the mattress on his bed depress, as if someone had sat down beside him. It sounded like a nightmare, and Ann dismissed it as such. But two months later, she would reconsider that conclusion.

Ann was lying awake in bed, one evening, when it happened.

"I noticed a man, standing in our bedroom doorway," she said, "wearing only a pair of undershorts, and pointing a pistol at us."

When Ann woke her husband, the intruder vanished, and although they checked the house thoroughly, no sign of him could be found.

"About two weeks later, the figure appeared again," Ann wrote. This time, however, the ghost had taken the time to make himself presentable. He materialized before Ann in a blue suit and white shirt. If there still was any question about whether the tall, blond, blue-eyed stranger was of this earth, it must have been answered on this occasion by the glowing halo that surrounded his head.

It was to be the last appearance for quite some time. Life in the Nelson home returned to normal when Ann's mother from Manitoba came to visit.

About a week before she was to return home, the women were enjoying a leisurely second cup of coffee at the breakfast table when Ann's mother blurted out a secret.

"Annie, I have something to tell you," she said. "I don't want to scare you, but there have been a few times here I felt someone sitting on my bed — and *something* was in the closet."

Ann immediately recalled her son's "nightmares" and shuddered. Her mother had been sleeping in young Jim's bedroom. The suspected ghost had never been mentioned to her.

"That evening, I told my husband that as much as I loved our home, I wanted to move. He agreed. The house sold within a month, and we bought another home in Burnaby."

Nearly a year later, Ann and her husband decided to take a drive back to Georgia Street and visit some of their old neighbours. Over coffee, the Nelsons' friends admitted being curious about their sudden departure. When Ann and her husband confessed that they believed their old house to be haunted, their friends' reaction was strong.

"It was my brother who used to live there," the man said, "but he's gone now. He was killed in a head-on collision two years ago."

Ann asked if the man had a photograph of his brother. He brought out a picture of eleven men, taken the night before his brother died. Ann didn't need to ask which one he was. She pointed to the tall, slim man with blonde hair and blue eyes.

"That's him," she said. "That's the ghost."

The Nelsons' friend, who was dark and plump and bore no resemblance to his brother, whatsoever, was shocked. Ann had never met his brother — indeed, never knew he existed — yet had just picked him out of an extensive line-up.

For Ann Nelson, the mystery of the house on Georgia Street had ended.

*****

Ghosts frequently seem to be the result of a sudden death, and it is theorized that in these cases, the spirit does not realize that the body has expired. If this was the cause of Ann Nelson's ghost, it would explain some of his behaviour.

When the spectre appeared in his underwear, brandishing a pistol, he was probably only reacting to the Nelsons' presence. Unaware that he had died, and that others had moved into his house, the man must have been terrified to wake up one night and find his home filled with strangers. What seemed to be a threatening action on the ghost's part was very likely a show of fear and self-defense.

The Doppelganger

The year was 1892. The place, Victoria. It was a delightfully warm summer evening, and the small group of people standing at the corner of Government and Fort streets were enjoying the mild weather and each other's company as they waited for the next street car to happen along.

As the trolley approached their intersection, however, a sudden panic prevailed. The men and women were horrified to see the easily recognizable finance minister, J.H. Turner, step off the curb and directly into the trolley's path. He seemed completely unaware of the huge vehicle about to mow him down.

There were screams of warning. The driver made a frantic attempt to stop the car, but there simply was not enough time. The tram struck Turner in the side, full force — and then, unbelievably, appeared to pass right through him. The man continued walking as if nothing had happened.

The crowd was astounded. They all agreed upon what they had seen, yet how could it be? It was a strange case, and due to get stranger.

Among the witnesses that evening was a journalist by the name of David W. Higgins. Higgins fancied himself a student of the occult, and had recorded several personal paranormal experiences. He thought he might count this among them and, the next day, hurried to get the finance minister's side of the story.

Upon seeing Turner, he immediately congratulated him on his narrow escape from death. The minister looked puzzled. When Higgins recounted the events of the previous evening, Turner shook his head.

"I was not out of my house all last evening," Turner said, according to the January 26, 1969 edition of the *Daily Colonist*. "It must have been someone else."

175

Who was that someone else? Perhaps a "doppelganger," the ghostly double of a living person. Or possibly the finance minister was having a sort of out-of-body experience — physically resting at home, while his spirit roamed the streets of Victoria. The apparition may have merely been a Turner look-alike, but that still leaves the mystery of how the street car passed through the man, without so much as attracting his attention.

Presumably, David W. Higgins' interest in the paranormal led him to be well versed on the subject, but even he could not settle on a theory. When he wrote of the experience a dozen years later, he admitted to being as "deeply puzzled" as ever about what transpired.

*****

There is one other tale from Victoria involving a street car and an apparition — and while it is less detailed, it is more disturbing.

This strange story took place one night in the 1920s as the Number Six trolley rattled along Fairfield Road, past the gates of the Ross Bay Cemetery. Very suddenly, a man appeared directly ahead of the street car. The driver tried desperately to stop in time, but he could not avoid hitting the pedestrian. He was horrified to see the man's bloody, mutilated body thrown to the side of the tracks.

As soon as the vehicle screeched to a stop, the driver jumped out and ran back along the rails — but he could find no body, no blood, no sign of the accident whatsoever.

Whether the pedestrian was a ghost or hallucination, the poor driver must have been haunted for years by the grisly image of his violent end.

*****

It often seems that a haunting is the psychic residue or imprint left upon a place.

The cause is sometimes as simple as years of repetitive behaviour. One British Columbia family lived, for years, with a grandparent who was in the habit of getting out of bed at a certain time to fix herself some tea and toast. Long after her death, at that same hour, the family would hear the old woman's slippers shuffling into the kitchen as she went for her snack.

The phenomena may also be the result of one event bearing tremendous emotional impact. Unfortunately, incidents that dramatic are seldom pleasant, and so, many hauntings are the unhappy legacy of tragic or violent circumstances.

In an old house on Bell Road in Surrey, a woman is reported to have hanged herself in the attic. Although she has been dead for years, tenants in the house frequently hear the crash of a stool being kicked away. It is a constant reminder of the woman's final, desperate act.

The most traumatic circumstance, however, must be murder. In the following three stories, rage and terror seem to have combined to create an apparition — a paranormal, visual record of the crime as it was committed.

The Party Scene

It was the mid-1930s during the height of the Depression. But on one particular evening in one particular house in an affluent Vancouver neighbourhood, there was no evidence of the country's economic woes. There was a party in progress and, for this occasion, no expense had been spared.

Fresh flowers decorated several highly polished tables, and elegant, tapered candles glowed on the mantle. Everyone complimented the hostess on her marvellous canapés, and the host on his choice of wine. There was music and laughter and, as the evening hours slipped by, it was obvious that the gathering was a smashing success.

It was surprising, then, when the mood of the group changed abruptly, just after midnight. The conversation ended all at once, and a number of guests shivered as the room seemed to cool several degrees.

Something strange was about to happen.

When the young couple first purchased the house, they thought it attractive and perfectly suited to their needs. After living there only a short time, however, both husband and wife felt uncomfortable and restless in the home. The atmosphere seemed wrong, and the only apparent solution was to renovate the structure extensively, thereby making it more "their own."

The project was a large and expensive one. Rugs and furniture were replaced. Paint and wallpaper were carefully selected and applied. Entire walls were taken out on the main floor, eliminating the master bedroom where the couple felt the most uneasy. The change created a lovely, open, and very large drawing room, where the young home-owners held their party celebrating the completion of the renovations. It was in this room that the strange chill descended, as the gathering moved into the morning hours.

No one broke the silence but, for some reason, every person in attendance felt obliged to focus their attention on the far end of the large room; the area that had once been the master bedroom. There was a collective gasp, as it became apparent why.

It was a scene that would remain unmercifully vivid in their memories, forever.

The original owners of the house had been a middle-aged couple. The woman was friendly and charming; the man, a definite loner. Neighbours found him difficult to approach and impossible to engage, as he refused all social invitations.

Less than a year after they moved in, the wife died suddenly. According to her husband, she had an existing heart condition. The authorities accepted this information and asked few further questions. They simply listed "heart failure" as the cause of death.

The man's grief seemed obvious. He immediately sold the house to the young couple and moved away — to escape painful memories, everyone assumed. The only odd behaviour was his firm refusal to leave a forwarding address. His reasons remained a mystery, until the night of the young couple's party.

The main-floor master bedroom was the room where the original lady of the house had died. It was the room that the young couple felt most uncomfortable in. And, even with the walls knocked out, it was the area that seemed to demand the attention of the party guests, that evening.

As they all stared, the air seemed to shimmer. Suddenly, a shape began to form. It was the apparition of a huge, four-poster bed. On it, lay a woman. She appeared stricken, and was very obviously struggling for breath. Worse, was the expression of terror she wore. Her pleading eyes were fixed on the man who sat calmly at her bedside. He seemed oblivious to her pain and, in fact, had a smug little smile on his face.

One of the witnesses to this horrifying vision was a woman who lived in the neighbourhood and had known the previous owners of the house. As the apparition faded, she broke the silence, exclaiming that the woman in the bed had been the one who died on that very spot. The man beside her had been her husband.

The group sat, shocked and speechless, suddenly aware that the cause of the lady's death had not been so natural, after all.

The grim scene, quite obviously, broke up the party. It also prompted the young couple to move immediately and sell the house and all its contents. The new, carefully selected furnishings, carpets and various ornaments went directly to an auction house.

While the property was being swiftly disposed of, an agreement was made among all those who witnessed the horrid phenomena. As they were sure no one would believe them, they agreed to keep their frightening experience a secret. Thus, the episode was efficiently put behind them.

One of the women was slightly more reluctant to let the issue go, however. Her curiosity drew her to the auction sale of the house's furnishings, where she found a shocking confirmation of the murder scene she had observed at the party.

As the woman browsed through the items for sale, she found herself drawn to a rug, taken from the room where the apparition was seen. What she saw amazed her.

The carpet had been much too new to be marked by the weight of anything that sat on it — yet there, in the deep pile, were four, deep, distinct indentations. They were set out in a large rectangle. They formed the shape of a four-poster bed.

In *Some Canadian Ghosts* (1973), Sheila Hervey wrote that following the incident at the party, there were never any reports or rumours of strange events in the house.

It was as if the single, powerful apparition had used all the energy available to impress itself upon the party-goers. Today, a large apartment block stands on the site of this experience and only two of the guests are alive to confirm the story.

But oh, what a story it is.

The Suspect Returns

The man's name was Jim Hawthornthwaite and, in the early 1900s, he was a member of British Columbia's Legislative Assembly. He made his living as a politician, and his home in Nanaimo, where he shared a house with a fellow by the name of Arthur Potts.

One evening, Potts heard a commotion in the living room, and went rushing in to see what was happening. There, he found Hawthornthwaite, wild-eyed and alone, waving a fireplace poker in a defensive arc.

"Did you see him?" the politician raved. "Where did he go?"

Potts assured his friend that he had seen no one leave the room, then cautiously asked what had happened. Hawthornthwaite proceeded to describe a grisly and dramatic scene, claiming he was confronted by a native man who was covered in blood and brandishing a gore-smeared axe.

It is not known whether Potts believed the wild story, but the house-mates never spoke to each other of the incident, again. In fact, it was years before Hawthornthwaite breathed another word about his fright — but when he did, he found a receptive ear.

It was Nanaimo's Chief of Police who had somehow inspired the retelling of this strange tale. Perhaps, over time, Hawthornthwaite had begun to doubt his own sanity, or perhaps he expected to be greeted with the chief's mocking scepticism, but he relayed the story in a somewhat apologetic, disclaiming tone. However, the politician's seeming lack of credulity did nothing to dampen the other man's enthusiastic interest.

As Bert Binny wrote in the April 27, 1958 edition of Victoria's *Daily Colonist*:

The description of the Indian, his appearance and the setting provided an exact replica of the scene and character when an Indian had been taken into custody in that very room some years previously.

He had murdered his wife with an axe.

It was one for the paranormal record books. The politician had been telling the truth.

The Reverse Ghost

She must have been a horrible sight.

In the mid-1970s, visitors to Beacon Hill Park in Victoria began seeing a disturbing apparition of a young woman in some bushes along a hillside.

The girl had long blond hair, was dressed in white slacks, and had dark, tanned skin. Her face was eternally twisted in a silent scream, and she held her arms out before her, as if to ward off an unseen threat. The terror in her eyes was apparent and distressing to all who saw her. Witnesses had to wonder how this poor girl had met her end.

The interesting thing was, she, as yet, had not.

In the fall of 1983, in that very grove of bushes, police made a sad discovery. It was the body of a young woman who had been missing for some months. The woman, apparently murdered, had long dark hair, pale skin and was dressed in dark denim jeans. Ghosts occasionally appear as photographic negatives and, if this was the case, the victim matched the image seen at that site for eight years previous. In *A Gathering of Ghosts* (1989), Robin Skelton and Jean Kozocari examine the mystery:

> The screaming ghost of Beacon Hill Park foretold the future. It is hard to determine, however, whether the young woman herself, by a kind of astral projection, was foreseeing her own death, or whether, by a curious twist in time, the place prerecorded a memory before the event had occurred.

The only certainty is this: since the murder of the unfortunate woman, there have been no known sightings of the spectre in Beacon Hill Park.

CHAPTER TEN

The "Explained"

For every ghost story that survives incredulous inspection, there are several for which explanations are found. Generally, they fall into two categories: deliberate cons or pranks, and coincidence or natural causes of seemingly supernatural effects.

When it came to deliberately creating illusions of the paranormal, few were as expert as the so-called spirit mediums of the early part of this century. The mysterious sounds and sights in a darkened séance room could usually be attributed to nothing more than clever stagecraft.

Tambourines and towels would be treated with glowing phosphorus and suspended in the air for eerie effect. Tables could be made to "float," when the medium's foot provided a little lift from beneath. Those who were truly dedicated to their craft would even swallow several feet of cheesecloth, to be regurgitated later as "an ectoplasmic manifestation."

But fakery has never been limited to the séance room.

Taking advantage of the public's eagerness to believe, a number of evangelists and faith healers have worked with concealed earphones and backstage assistants to create the illusion of receiving messages from God. And showboat psychics have often been able to captivate television audiences with their amazing abilities to bend metal and manipulate objects when, in fact, they were often relying on old-fashioned magicians' sleight of hand.

Even away from the spotlight, the urge to trick people into believing the unbelievable is common. Every child who ever took part in an amateur séance at a sleep-over knows how to secretly push the Ouija planchette or tap on the wall when nobody's looking.

But, more common than the cons, are the coincidences; the many times it is discovered that a scraping tree branch or expanding hot-water pipe made the mysterious noise, that marsh gas created the eerie glow over the graveyard, or that headlights from the street caused a shadowy shape to swoop across the room.

There are the fools and there are the frauds ... Scouring British Columbia's abundance of ghost folklore unearthed one famous example of each.

The Ross Bay Mistake

No one could blame the witnesses; after all, people *expect* a cemetery to be haunted. But it wasn't Hallowe'en, when the imaginations of young people are ripe with images of spectres — this was one Christmas Eve in the 1920s, and ghosts and goblins should have been far from everyone's minds.

Two young girls who were walking home decided to take a short-cut through the Ross Bay Cemetery. It was early evening, and darkness had fallen. Suddenly, one girl froze in her tracks. She clutched at her friend's sleeve and pointed to a spot several yards away.

"Look!" she whispered frantically. "Do you see it?"

It would have been hard not to. There, rising from behind a weathered tombstone was a filmy, white apparition. It glowed ethereally against the black night sky and flitted away across the graveyard.

The girls needed to see no more. They spun around and ran back the way they came, arriving, breathless and pale, on Fairfield Road. A street car had stopped there to collect passengers and, as the girls gasped out the story of their fright, several men and women nodded excitedly. They had seen the spirit, too, while waiting for the tram. The conductor, who had been bringing the car to a stop at the time, also concurred.

Had the story come only from two schoolgirls, it would likely have not lasted. But considering there were so many witnesses, most of them responsible adult citizens, the tale of the Ross Bay Cemetery ghost proved enduring and credible. In fact, it would be twenty full years before anyone solved the mystery.

It is said the truth came to light when several people who were waiting in a long theatre line began to discuss the years-old legend of the Ross Bay ghost. Some believed the tale; others didn't. Then, one old fellow stepped forward with an entirely new perspective. He said he *was* the Ross Bay ghost, and proceeded with an explanation.

The man claimed that he and a friend had been unemployed during that particular Christmas season, so many years before. To make a little money for the holidays, they devised a plan: they would buy a bit of gold leaf paint, and restore the lettering on some of the more worn headstones in the Ross Bay Cemetery. They were sure the families of the deceased would happily pay for such a service — and they were correct. The men made a nice bit of holiday cash but, in order to collect it, had to complete the work before Christmas.

On December 24th, the friends were working feverishly, trying to finish their commissions. As the sun set, they resorted to working by flashlight. As the wind picked up, they covered themselves with sheets to protect the expensive gold leaf paint.

And the rest almost writes itself.

About 7:00 p.m., just as the young girls were beginning to cross the cemetery and the street car was rattling up to its stop, there was a mighty gust of wind. It picked up the container of expensive paint one man was working with, and sent it rolling across the ground. Panicked at the thought of losing his investment, the fellow jumped up, ignoring the fact that he was tangled in the billowy white sheet he had been using to shelter himself, and tried to chase the paint down. The flashlight he carried beneath the cloth created the luminescence, and completed the spectral effect.

It ended with a maddeningly rational explanation — but for two decades, the legend of the Ross Bay Cemetery was one of Victoria's finest ghost stories.

The Haunting of the St. George Hotel

In the January 26, 1969 edition of Victoria's *Daily Colonist*, reporter T.W. Paterson began a ghost story by writing, "This is one of the briefest cases on record, having lasted but a night ..."

How right he was. The haunting of Victoria's St. George Hotel was ever so brief — the ghost was discovered to be a fraud, within hours — still, it makes an entertaining tale.

It began when a woman registered at the hotel and booked the dining room, where she planned a demonstration of her amazing psychic prowess. She promised to astound and delight her audience with, among other accomplishments, her ability to "read" a closed book.

A volume would be placed in her hands, and a member of the audience would quote a passage from it. Without opening the pages, the woman was strangely able to announce the exact number of the page upon which that quote would be found.

The audience tested the woman several times, using a collection of Shakespeare's works and the New Testament. Every time, she answered correctly and with ease. But, just as she was beginning to look infallible, someone produced a book of their own. At that moment, the woman's uncanny ability seemed to vanish and she was forced to retreat, red-faced with embarrassment.

Most in attendance were left believing that the woman's talent was not clairvoyance but, rather, a phenomenal memory. This being fascinating in itself, it seems strange that she didn't promote herself more honestly — but her actions later in the evening suggest that she was, perhaps, a bit obsessed with the paranormal.

Late that night in the St. George Hotel, mysterious things began to take place. Odd knocking sounds were heard on the doors and walls and bells rang in places where no bell was known to exist. Low, hollow moans floated through the empty hotel hallways — but stopped immediately, when the manager and his wife put on their robes and ventured out to investigate.

The couple was standing in the hall outside their own suite when they glimpsed a tall, white figure gliding along the dimly lit passage. When it disappeared at the head of the staircase, the manager shook himself out of his state of shock and gave chase.

When he reached the spot where the ghost had vanished, he discovered a rumpled bed sheet on the floor. Instantly, he understood that his "spirit" was of the flesh and blood variety and, given the earlier hoax of the evening, he knew just where to start looking for it.

The manager and his wife went immediately to the "psychic" reader's room. They pounded on the door for several minutes before the woman finally opened it, yawning as if she had been dragged from a deep sleep.

The manager flew into an angry speech, demanding an explanation for the woman's behaviour, while she vehemently denied his accusations. The manager's wife used a silent approach, which proved to be ultimately more effective. She simply marched into the hotel room, threw back the bed cover, and proved her case — with a mattress that was one sheet short of its full complement. The missing sheet was the one discarded by the "ghost," in the hallway.

Twice humiliated, the so-called psychic checked out the very next morning, taking her show to the next unsuspecting town. And, as for the St. George Hotel, it was never haunted again.

Bibliography

BOOKS

Anderson, Frank W. 1989. *69 Interesting Places in Central British Columbia.* Saskatoon: Gopher Books.

Belyk, Robert C. 1990. *Ghosts.* Ganges, British Columbia: Horsdal & Schubart Publishers Ltd.

Broughton, Richard S. 1991. *Parapsychology; The Controversial Science.* New York: Ballantine Books.

Colombo, John Robert. 1991. *Mackenzie King's Ghost.* Toronto: Hounslow Press.

Colombo, John Robert. 1988. *Mysterious Canada.* Toronto: Doubleday Canada Limited.

Guiley, Rosemary Ellen. 1991. *Harper's Encyclopedia of Mystical and Paranormal Experience.* New York: HarperCollins Publishers.

Hervey, Sheila. 1996. *Canada Ghost to Ghost.* Toronto: Stoddart Publishing Company Ltd.

Hervey, Sheila. 1973. *Some Canadian Ghosts.* Richmond Hill, Ontario: Simon and Schuster of Canada, Ltd.

Moberly, C.A.E., and E.F. Jourdain. 1911. *An Adventure.* London, England: Faber and Faber.

Reksten, Terry. 1987. *Craigdarroch; The Story of Dunsmuir Castle.* Victoria, British Columbia: Orca Book Publishers.

Reksten, Terry. 1991. *The Dunsmuir Saga.* Vancouver: Douglas & McIntyre.

Reksten, Terry. 1978. *Rattenbury.* Victoria, British Columbia: Sono Nis Press.

Skelton, Robin and Jean Kozocari. 1989. *A Gathering of Ghosts.* Saskatoon: Western Producer Prairie Books.

Sonin, Eileen. 1970. *ESP-ecially Ghosts.* Toronto: Clarke, Irwin & Company Limited.

Woodcock, George. 1990. *British Columbia, A History of the Province.* Vancouver: Douglas & McIntyre.

The Editors of Time-Life Books. 1989. *Hauntings.* Alexandria, Virginia: Time-Life Books Inc.

The Editors of Time-Life Books. 1988. *Phantom Encounters.* Alexandria, Virginia: Time-Life Books Inc.

The Editors of Time-Life Books. 1989. *Spirit Summonings.* Alexandria, Virginia: Time-Life Books Inc.

ARCHIVAL SOURCES

Chilliwack Museum & Historical Society

Samuel Roy Cromarty; Oral History

PERIODICALS

Boundary Creek Times: February 22, 1995.

Courtenay Comox Valley *Record:* December 9, 1987.

Entertainment Weekly: "The X-Files Exposed," by Dana Kennedy, March 10, 1995.

Gulf Islands Driftwood: January 25, 1995.

Journal of the American Society for Psychical Research: "Direct Contacts with Past and Future: Retrocognition and Precognition," by Gardner Murphy, January 1967.

Kootenay Review: July 1993.

Ladysmith-Chemainus Chronicle: February 21, 1995.

Lakes District News: February 22, 1995.

New York Times: November 10, 1901.

Quesnel *Advocate:* January 25, 1995.

Sooke Mirror: November 15, 1989.

Two Worlds: March 5, 1955.

Vancouver *Province:* April 9, 1964; May 30 and 31, 1966; June 9 and 24, 1966; March 31, 1973; December 23, 1976; October 14, 1980; and December 15, 1985.

Vancouver Sun: July 21, 1945; June 3 and 6, 1966; December 23, 1976; October 31, 1986; and October 31, 1987.

Victoria *Daily Colonist:* September 29 and 30, 1936; October 27, 1936; March 23, 1958; April 6 and 27, 1958; May 19, 1968; January 26, 1969; and September 23, 1979.

Victoria *Times-Colonist:* November 26, 1989; and November 4, 1995.

WHERE Victoria: "A-Haunting We Will Go," by Kirsten Meincke, October, 1994.